CH01024949

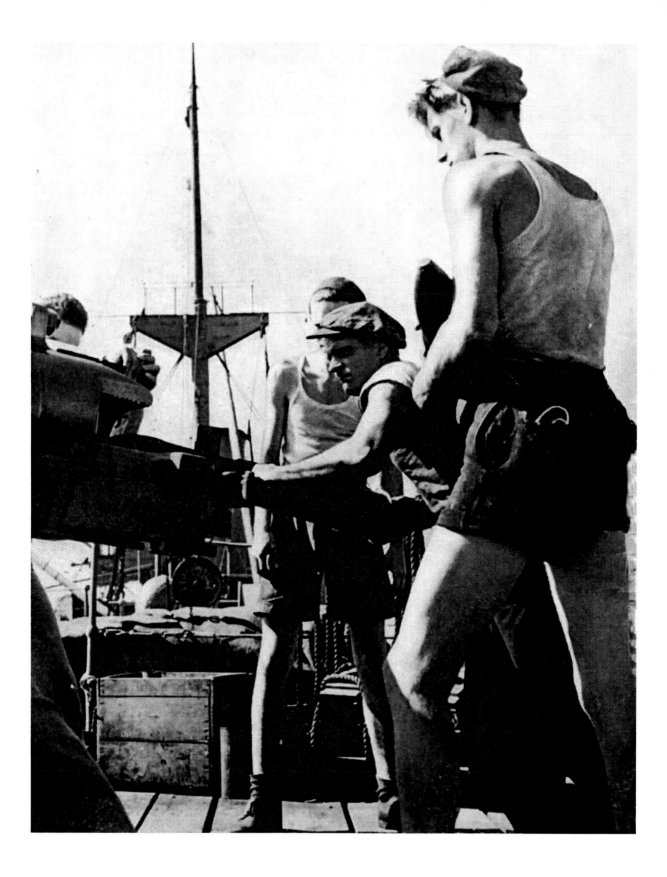

MERCHANTMEN AT WAR

The Official Story of the Merchant Navy: 1939-1944

Prepared for the Ministry of War Transport
by the Ministry of Information

University Press of the Pacific
Honolulu, Hawaii

Merchantmen at War:
The Official Story of the Merchant Navy: 1939-
1944

by
UK Ministry of Information

for the UK Ministry of War Transport

ISBN: 1-4102-2359-0

Reprinted from the 1944 edition

University Press of the Pacific
Honolulu, Hawaii
http://www.universitypressofthepacific.com

FOR ALL SEAFARERS

Even in peace, scant quiet is at sea ;
In war, each revolution of the screw,
Each breath of air that blows the colours free,
May be the last life movement known to you.

Death, thrusting up or down, may disunite
Spirit from body, purpose from the hull,
With thunder, bringing leaving of the light,
With lightning letting nothingness annul.

No rock, no danger, bears a warning sign,
No lighthouse scatters welcome through the dark ;
Above the sea, the bomb ; afloat, the mine ;
Beneath, the gangs of the torpedo-shark.

Year after year, with insufficient guard,
Often with none, you have adventured thus ;
Some, reaching harbour, maimed and battle-scarred
Some, never more returning, lost to us.

But, if you 'scape, tomorrow, you will steer
To peril once again, to bring us bread,
To dare again, beneath the sky of fear,
The moon-moved graveyard of your brothers dead.

You were salvation to the army lost,
Trapped, but for you, upon the Dunkirk beach ;
Death barred the way to Russia, but you crosst ;
To Crete and Malta, but you succoured each.

Unrecognized, you put us in your debt ;
Unthanked, you enter, or escape, the grave ;
Whether your land remember or forget
You saved the land, or died to try to save.

JOHN MASEFIELD

CONTENTS

With two poems specially written for this book by the Poet Laureate:

THE MAPS

There are many men and women in the Forces, who would welcome a chance of reading this book. If you hand it in to the nearest Post Office, it will go to them.

THE story of the Merchant Navy in this war is a story of battles ; every convoy that successfully reaches port is a battle won.

Those successful battles number many hundreds, perhaps thousands. For each convoy that has suffered loss since the war started, two or three have reached harbour intact, having overcome the sea's natural hazards, and, from time to time, the perils of mine, submarine torpedo, aerial bomb and shells from the surface raider. They have achieved this through the men's own seamanship and courage, but those qualities would not have availed without the constant guard of the Royal Navy, protecting them not only when in convoy, but routeing them along the safest sea lanes, and keeping a close eye on each liner or fast cargo ship sailing alone across the oceans. Moreover, as the war has developed, the Royal Air Force has flown farther and farther to guard our ships until by the spring of 1943 it was penetrating more than a thousand miles from Britain across the Atlantic. These Coastal Command aircraft, with others flying from Canada and from Iceland, and working in company with Fleet Air Arm aircraft from escort carriers, closed at last the mid-Atlantic gulf.

Our merchant seamen have been in the war from the beginning. Only nine hours after hostilities began, the Donaldson liner *Athenia* (Captain J. Cook), sailing to the United States with 1,418 men, women and children, was torpedoed without warning 200 miles off the Irish coast, with the loss of 112 people, 19 of them members of the crew. It was the signal that the enemy would fight at sea without law and without mercy.

From that time the war at sea has never ceased , it is unlikely to do so till the end is reached. There have been lulls on land but seldom on, over, or below the waters. Our merchant officers and seamen have suffered casualties, at times so grievous as to be much greater than the contemporary losses in the armed forces. Their triumph is that they have never been daunted ; ships have not been kept in harbour by the perils outside. Some of their sailing conditions have seldom been matched in the previous history of our merchant seamen. On winter convoys to Murmansk and Archangel officers and men when on deck have dressed like Arctic explorers, and the ship has often laboured under an extra burden of 150 tons of ice. Days that are almost totally dark have been punctuated by attacks from U-boats, and days that have barely any darkness at all by attacks from torpedo-bombers numbering, on one convoy, 42 attacks in three days.

To Malta, sometimes called " the classic convoy ", our merchant ships voyaged when nothing short of battleships and aircraft carriers could get them through and when air attacks were as certain as the dawn, noon and sunset, and as heavy as those on our cities. To Suez via the Cape on a 12,000-mile journey our cargo ships have sailed with the regularity of mail trains. Across the Atlantic they have voyaged, peopling those 2,000 miles of sea with maybe a dozen mighty convoys at a time, as though nothing worse than squalls or fog and snow lurked there. Narvik, Dunkirk, Singapore, Tobruk, Rangoon, Algiers, Casablanca—all these saw the Red Ensign at the perilous hour. Ships have often carried cargoes they were never built

for, in seas they were never meant to sail, over routes at times so devious that it appeared as though a malign spirit had carefully chosen the longest way round. But wherever our ships have been, their duty has been the same—to carry food, raw materials and armaments, and take the troops to their appointed places.

Our merchantmen bring us at least one-third (in weight) of our food, including most of our meat, butter, cheese and wheat. Nor could our own farmers raise their crops without the aid of fertilisers from overseas. As for our raw materials, the swiftest glance at them shows how our life is built on the sea. Steel and timber from North America, wool from Australia and New Zealand, nitrates from South America, iron ore from Spain and West Africa, cotton from North and South America, Egypt and India, zinc and lead from North America and Australia, oil from America and Persia. And as the merchant fleets have maintained this base which is Britain, so have they taken forth our armies and their material to the foreign fields on which they have fought. Every blow we deliver is firmly linked with the sea and seamen. Let us take one example —the bombers which are crushing the enemy's power at its source ; for a 500-bomber raid on Germany by four-engine aircraft we need 750,000 gallons of fuel oil— oil that is seaborne to Britain.

THE MEN OF THE MERCHANT NAVY

1. The Sea is their Trade

HE went to sea at the age of $15\frac{1}{2}$, and that was 53 years ago; he is still at sea. This indeed is his third war spent so, for he was second mate of a troopship when the soldiers hanging over his rail were off to fight the Boers. He is a short, thick-set man, with a face stern of line, but his brown eye has humour in it. He puts his feet down with deliberation, as though he had better be firm with a floor that may shift a trifle as he moves over it. If you ask him whether this war at sea is much worse than the last, he says well, of course, the bombers and torpedo bombers have brought new dangers and problems, and he doesn't remember that the U-boats in the last war worked in anything more than couples, whereas now. . . . But the sea, he says, was always hazardous and these are merely new hazards. The regular merchant seaman is a disciplined man (he says) and takes the ordeals easier than an ordinary man would; the sea is his trade—he knows nothing else. He himself was at sea when the war broke out and it wasn't

long before he got word of a ship being torpedoed; so he steered his ship for the scene, not so much because he thought he'd find survivors, but because he took it that would be a spot the U-boats would have departed from. He was right: he made port. Since then he has crossed the Atlantic many times.

Off his ship you find him wearing a blue serge suit and a blue mackintosh and a trilby hat. He seems a little out of his element; he is very courteous, and there is a touch of shyness in him, though he has a high opinion of his dignity and importance. There is a fine dryness in his yarns; the yarn, for instance, about a Master who was fond of saying that a thing is not lost if you know where it is, which led to his steward remarking: " Well, sir, that makes it easier to tell you where your silver teapot is—I dropped it accidentally over the side ".

This ship's Master is typical of the merchant service, a service which dislikes fuss of any sort, and takes the war to a considerable degree in its stride. He is of the old school, has his square-rig ticket (not many Masters with this particular distinction are still at sea), and he could tell of boyhood days when a ship's biscuit had thirteen holes in it and a weevil poked its head out of every one.

THESE MEN ARE A BROTHERHOOD. THEY KNOW SHIPS, STORM, ICE, FOG, SUBMARINE, SURFACE-RAIDER, BOMBER

Our Merchant Navy, however, has as many sorts of Masters as a stock exchange has stockbrokers, and as many sorts of seamen as a coal-pit has hewers of coal. There are the liner crews, proud of their ships and uniforms, and there are men on tramps who'll say : " What ? Me on a liner, washing paint all day and dressed-up like a May horse ? Oh, no ! " But they are alike in this—they're fond of a discussion ; they will read an old newspaper and digest a subject and develop an argument about it ; they will growl about their grievances as a soldier will, and they will harbour superstititions. The bulk of them nurture a belief in Divine Providence, as is natural enough among men who endure both the malice and the kindliness of the sea. But as for describing them, one can do no more than run over those who have fixed themselves in the memory.

There is the old Master in his fiftieth year at sea who said that he was once a marksman at Bisley and finds, when he puts three bullets from his Ross rifle into a Focke-Wulf's cockpit, " She don't stay " ; another Master is a youngish man not much bigger than a jockey who said his friends call him Gordon Richards ; a third was a Scotsman wearing his gold-leafed cap and a white silk muffler who said with relish, " I'm not a Yes-man, I'm a No-man " ; a fourth, Master of a troopship, a giant with a hooked nose and glinting eye, said he always turns into his bed at sea now, though in the war's first year he never did ; a fifth, who walked on his ship wearing a brown suit and trilby hat, said he had sailed tankers throughout the last war and this, and until his last voyage had not seen anything of the enemy ; a sixth, burly man with eyes almost violet in colour, who has many thousands of lives in his keeping, says he has a jolly disposition but sails keyed up so that he can sometimes hear a whistle on the bridge when nobody else can. There is the Master who says the last war was a picnic compared with this, for the last " had no metal in it to speak of " and once well away from Britain you had no need to worry about submarines, but now, bless your soul, the farther you are off the worse it is. There is the Commodore captain of 67 who, when asked if he would care to make a voyage or two, replied : " Letter received. Very pleased. Go anywhere, any time ".

The Clyde, the north-east coast, South Wales, Liverpool, Whitby, Hull, the West Country—time and time again it is from one of these that our ships' Masters and men have sprung. Any town in the British Isles may produce seamen ; but the smell of the sea and the sight of water and of ships have their own inspiration. Men and boys who have stared long hours to a far horizon are likely to be those who seek what lies beyond. Moreover, the phrase " sea in his blood " can be a true one ; the seafarer's is a trade—like many another—that runs in families.

The sea breeds a calmness in facing hazards so that our seamen of long apprenticeship are inclined to be imperturbable men ; and not only the Masters. There was the tanker's chief officer with eyes as blue and wide open as a baby's—a Newcastle man. He smiled and drank his tea and said : " Now these U-boats—you lose 'em in the morning and they're back at night. They *were* in packs but now they're in schools. Well, you're lucky or you're unlucky—that's how I look at it, anyhow ". He sleeps with a small axe at his bedside so that his hand will fall on it, for no man knows when such a tool will be needed. His chief engineer, 30 or so, growing a downy beard, was a man who seemed to be tickled by the way the orders for changing speed come to him—" Five up or five down. Sometimes they'll say, ' Five up,' and that's a sub. away " (meaning we've sunk one). He chuckled again and went on to say those are the best engines he's had—he wouldn't like anything to happen to those engines.

Go from ship to ship and a fair proportion of the men you meet are noteworthy : the troopship chef who says it was so hot in the Red Sea that his wooden spoon was set alight as he made the salmon mayonnaise ; the young bos'n of 28 with a hundred men under him, doing work that is usually done by a grizzled, hard-bitten man of middle-age ; the dark, gentle youth who was torpedoed when working as a steward and said at the time : " No more sea for me ", but has been getting restive and is off back because, he says, " shore seems tame after a while " ; the steward of the *Georgic* who won the D.S.C. at Gallipoli and had been a trumpeter under Bindon Blood in the Boer War and served in the Foreign Legion in between ; the apprentice who understudied Sonnie Hale and who entertained the lads in mid-Atlantic over the loudspeaker ; the chief engineer of a benzine tanker—a broad-faced man from Sunderland—who said it's really not so bad on a tanker because half her time she's in ballast carrying water in her tanks, and when so she's the safest thing afloat ; and there is Willie, the Scots cabin-boy aged $15\frac{1}{2}$, who sailed on Norwegian ships before he tried British. By all the official recommendations Willie ought not to be there at all ; boys under 16 should not be taken and, indeed, an endeavour is being made to raise the age to 17. But lads tramp to the docks and tramp round the ships, and men who may have run away to sea themselves are not likely to discourage boys seeking adventure. Our seamen may have changed in appearance, and young men sometimes go up for their officers' tickets wearing plus fours in place of the old-time double-breasted blue jacket and white collar ; but lads are still fired by the sea, nor will tales of hardship in open boats deter them. The Shipping Federation receives over a hundred letters a day from boys asking for work afloat.

When the war began, a large number of merchant officers and seamen went at once into the Royal Navy ; in all, about 12,000 of them, men who were either in the Royal Naval Reserve or were serving in vessels which became armed merchant cruisers, such as the *Jervis Bay*. The demand for merchant officers was so considerable that the Admiralty was asked by the Board of

Trade to go a trifle slow, if possible, in calling up senior officers.

The translation of merchant seamen into Royal Navy men was, of course, not a new development. The merchant ships and fishing fleets are one of the fighting ships' bulwarks in times of emergency. To-day there is probably no large naval ship that does not number R.N.R. officers in its complement, and at least one submarine is commanded by a former merchant officer, and countless small surface ships as well.

But it will be seen that the Merchant Navy suffered a diminution of manpower so soon as war broke out. The existing numbers were already less than could have been wished to face total war. British shipping had suffered gravely during the years of trade depression between the two wars. We had lived through a period in which some of our rivers and lochs were choked with laid-up ships, and many an officer was glad to go to sea in the fo'c'sle rather than walk the streets ; men had left the sea at the rate of 15,000 or more a year. Marine engineers found work ashore more readily than deck officers, and when war broke out hundreds of them were working near Southampton. This reservoir of officers, engineers and sea-men proved to be a source of great strength when the need arose.

Men of vision had seen, long before, that a Merchant Navy reserve was desirable in the event of war. In September 1938 the Government asked for volunteers willing to return to the sea if the need arose. The response was excellent ; on September 3rd, 1939, the actual enrolments were 12,785 and rose later to 23,107. Then fresh measures were adopted and in the spring of 1941, 59,000 officers and men registered their names as having served on ships since 1936. A host of them returned to the trade of the sea as volunteers. Of those who registered, 3,500 were navigating officers, 7,450 were engineers, 12,500 were deck ratings, 17,500 were engine-room ratings, and 13,500 had worked in catering departments.

FROM BOMBAY, FROM SIERRA LEONE, FROM MOMBASA

The actual size of the Merchant Navy's personnel, remembering the immense work it accomplishes, is comparatively small. Those who are British were estimated in June 1942 to number 120,000 (equal to about eight army divisions)—4,550 Masters, 12,950 deck officers, 19,800 engineers, 35,400 deck ratings, 29,900 engine-room ratings and 17,400 stewards.

The merchant seaman is a man of independence of mind and character. It suited him well in normal times to be paid off at the end of a voyage. If he wanted a spell ashore, he could have it ; if his wish was to sign on for a new part of the world, in a fresh sort of ship, nothing stood in his way—provided he found the ship ; both the South Seas and the Arctic were within his reach.

His discipline was of a free and easy sort, and spit-and-polish, apart from the big liners, seldom formed part of it. He wore what he liked in the ship and he wore what he liked ashore ; whether his shoes were black or yellow, his face shaved or not, his trousers dungarees or serge, his shirt rag or starched, was his own affair. He was a civilian and remains a civilian. When a ship's Master—and whether from tramp or liner makes little difference—gets into a British port, it is seldom long before he takes off his gold-laced *cap and his uniform and walks abroad in* mufti, not to be distinguished at a quick glance from the rest of us. His clothes may not be the latest cut, the roll in his gait may seem a little peculiar, but it will take a sharp eye to notice either. As for the seamen and firemen of to-day, the greasers, trimmers, donkeymen, stokers, carpenters and quartermasters, their faces may be red or browned by sun or touched with sallowness from the boiler-room, and their talk among themselves may be of the trip behind them and the one ahead. But in a crowd walking to a football match it would be hard to pick them out. Their clothes would not help. The small silver-coloured badge in their buttonhole lettered " M.N." is not very noticeable and, anyhow, not all of them wear it. Ashore,

the bulk of them, officers and men, feel a trifle out of their element, as though the region were uncharted and its occupants not entirely to be trusted.

Maybe it is not surprising, then, that for a year and three-quarters after the war began no marked change was made in the fashion of employing merchant seamen. They were reserved from the age of 18, but could leave the sea between voyages (for, having signed off, they were unemployed) and move from one reserved occupation to another, and sometimes they did so. The shore competed ; seamen whose families had suffered in the *blitz*, or were evacuated, often found other work to do. At the same time, since passenger traffic had declined, stewards became surplus and by the end of 1940 over 1,000 of them had been trained as deckhands. In spite of this, a shortage of A.B.s began to be felt, and of engineers also. By the end of 1940 ships were from time to time held up for crews. It was in May 1941, after consultation with the Shipping Federation and the officers' and men's representatives, that an Essential Work Order for the Merchant Navy was created, and the registration of seamen who had left the sea since 1936 was begun. The result was a revolution in sea industry employment. Seamen henceforth *could not leave the sea. On the other hand,* they are guaranteed pay between voyages, and also leave ; for every month of service on ship's articles, officers get two and a half days' leave and men two days'. What is known as " The Pool " was created. If, on leaving his ship, a man is at once re-engaged by the shipowner, he does not enter the pool ; but if not so re-engaged he joins the pool, and can be directed, when his leave is up, to another ship or to another port. So far as possible men serve in the types of ships they know, but this cannot always be arranged. The seaman must take the rough with the smooth. Quarters in old ships are much poorer than in new ones ; so are the cooking galleys. But he doesn't draw extra pay for poorly equipped ships or for dangerous

LEARNING THEIR TRADE The sea will be their lifelong school, but when in port they still take instruction from experienced Masters. These young recruits, being examined on board their ship, are working for their Efficiency Deck-Hand Certificate.

routes. Danger does not deter him, anyhow. Many a man has made more fuss over a dirty mattress than going to Archangel in winter. And when ships' boats were taken off vessels for North Africa that more landing craft might be carried, the seamen did not demur ; on the contrary, they said, " Don't coddle us. Treat us like soldiers ".

The seaman did not like " the Pool " at first—it interfered with his liberty—but he has begun to realise that it has its advantages and, taken in the round, it works well. The pool supplies 400 officers and 3,000 ratings a week ; it functions not only in this country but in ports overseas also.

As the war has progressed, men have been trained for the Merchant Navy, as others have been trained for the armed forces. Indeed, the Merchant Navy, through the Shipping Federation, has trained firemen for the first time in history, setting up schools at London, Cardiff and Newcastle-on-Tyne, where the men are taught the expert coaling of fires in order to maintain steam and prevent smoke issuing from the stack. The Royal Navy, which for a lengthy period had more volunteers than could be absorbed, began to train a number for our merchant ships ; several thousand have received a three months' naval course before sailing in merchantmen as deckhands. Gravesend Sea School has continued to train boys, turning out in 1942 the highest number since 1926. At one time there were as many as a further

1,000 waiting to enter that training school.

Thousands of men are serving in ships for the first time. Quite often they are shipmates with men who have grown old in the sea's service. Glance through any assembly of ships' articles and you'll find the names of engineers of 60 and over, perhaps a first-mate of 61, an assistant steward of 64, an A.B. of 66, and a fireman of a coal-burning ship of 62. A greaser is at sea aged 75. A steward who lost a leg in this war is back in a ship doing his old job. Other men have gone back to the sea after long absence. A Justice of the Peace growing crops in Orkney and Shetland, who had parted from ships 20 years before, returned to become second mate of the *Empire Dolphin*. The m.v. *Port Gisborne* had among her crew an able seaman who had left the sea while still a youth and, before returning as a deck-hand in this war, had run an hotel, owned hunters, achieved a " B " licence for flying and a 2-handicap at golf, sailed his 25-ton yawl to Monte Carlo and raced motor cars there. A third, who is a graduate of Cambridge, served in the Royal Navy in the last war and was mathematics master at a Perthshire college when he left to become a junior engineer in the Merchant Navy to-day.

The ranks of radio officers have swollen threefold during the war. To-day it is customary for every ship over 1,600 tons to carry three radio officers, some of them as young as 16 years of age. A reputation for devotion to duty, won in peace, has been more than maintained in war. Sometimes they have been the last to leave a ship and have sent out wireless messages to the end. When the *Graf Spee* on one occasion hoisted a notice on her bridge reading " Close your wireless or we shall shell you", the radio was not closed ; and when shelling began, and a fragment went through his cabin, the radio officer lay on the floor reaching up to his instrument with one arm, continuing what he had begun.

The crews of our merchantmen are not,

of course, all from the United Kingdom. Men from distant parts of the Commonwealth are alongside our own, rendering the same service, enduring the same dangers and hardships. Among these were 45,000 Indians when the war began. Moreover, there were over 6,000 Chinese and a considerable number of Arab firemen, all of them an integral part of the Merchant Navy. Of a lascar boy named Abdul Rahman in the s.s. *Auditur* (Captain E. Bennet, O.B.E.) the chief officer wrote that in an open boat he kept up men's spirits by telling stories and leading prayer meetings ; whenever a repair had to be done, as for instance to the heel of the mast, he did it all by himself ; and he kept at least six hours' watch each night. When the limited water ration was doled out, he always waited to the last.

Of Allied and neutral seamen serving with us, mostly under their own flags and laws, there are nearly 50,000.

Within the Merchant Navy itself a Master or seaman who looked back in the summer of 1944 to the war's beginning could see that, while much had remained immutable, much had changed. It was true that a number of ships 40 years old, overdue for retirement even before the war, still sailed the seas with men's quarters and galleys of which no modern eye could approve. But the changes were great, and most of them for the better. On the newly built ships a man gets 32 square feet of sleeping room against the 12 square feet he had prior to 1937 ; and, indeed, there are ships sailing now on which seamen are berthed two to a cabin, and in one or two ships they have a cabin each.

The training of cooks has kept some good food at all events from being spoilt in the galley, and airgraphs have kept many a seaman in touch with his wife when normal letters would not have done. For his hours ashore, over a hundred new clubs and canteens have been opened in ports overseas from Iceland to Capetown and Vancouver to Sydney. But all these are minor affairs compared with the improvements in life-saving described in a later chapter. One thing in particular is sometimes said: that the young seaman has come into his own, that he can set a course by the stars, and judge the approximate direction of wind without a compass by taking cloud formations and weather data for his only guides—a thing an older generation could not do. This at least is certain : that many a young seaman or apprentice has acquitted himself nobly in charge of a boatload of survivors ; . . . and this, too—that never in history have there been more applications from boys anxious to go to sea.

It has been said that it took the last war to give merchant officers a uniform and a standing they had never possessed before. To-day the British Merchant Navy ranks with any service in the world, armed or unarmed. It is by this time as tried and tested as the Royal Navy and as battle-experienced as either the Eighth or Second Armies.

---

2. Sailing Orders

BEFORE a deep-sea convoy sails, a conference is held between the Royal Navy and the merchant Masters, accompanied sometimes by their chief engineers or navigating officers. To this conference comes, where possible, the Commodore of Convoy.

" Well, gentlemen, any doubtful starters ? " With this colloquial phrase, used by the R.N. chairman, the conference begins. He stands and looks down the whitewashed room at the ships' captains, who within the next 24 hours will be setting off in convoy across the Atlantic. Gusts of April rain and wind strike the windows.

At the far end, models of aircraft are slung from the roof. Behind the chairman, a printed notice asks, " Have you got a blue bulb in your stern light ? " and another requests them to have two white rockets ready to fire. The atmosphere is easy and informal. Some of the Masters—among them Americans, Norwegians, Dutch and other Allies—are young ; several under 40. They are not all stamped with the sea. A number might be business men, or lawyers, or writers. In fact, we have Masters 27 years old, as we have Masters of 70 still at sea who joke about the depth of water they drew on Ararat. Not many are in uniform but a few wear blue mackintoshes over their civilian clothes. Attaché cases, rolled-up charts, documents and papers are spread before them. An onlooker could almost mistake this for a board meeting or a trade union meeting, were the half-dozen in uniform absent.

In reply to the chairman's question, a Master says that he is short of an engineer ; another, whose last voyage was to Murmansk, mentions there is a small repair being done, " but I think I'll be sailing", he adds quietly. The chairman next draws their attention to the manner of identifying themselves when at sea, and to the list of radio beacons on our coasts. " Just read that paragraph, please", he says, and there is a silence while they do so. " Is that clear ? " he continues, " now turn to your sailing orders, gentlemen "— these give the time of leaving, speed, distance between ships, etc. He tells them they must keep closed up on one another's tails when they pass through the gate (the boom). He refers to sheets of formation designs, and others headed " Stop Press". All convoys, he points out, may be used for practice attacks by our own aircraft, and gunlayers must be warned. In the same quiet, matter-of-fact tone, he remarks : " Any ship that straggles must remember she is in dangerous waters and may be sunk". If she is farther than a given number of degrees west, she should proceed to a certain route.

He has cheerful news for them also—there are new additional sea escorts other than the close escorts ; more long-range aircraft are coming into service which, as weather improves, will spend more days at sea. He describes a recent occasion when ten U-boats were operating near a convoy. Three were avoided, six others were attacked. Only one U-boat got through and she was depth-charged for two hours. He adds that submarines are normally working in packs up to 20.

Some Masters glance up through their spectacles, others lean back smoking their pipes, others turn their papers over busily.

A man whose stature resembles that of Lord Nelson now rises, wearing the uniform of a Commodore, R.N.R. He is 64, but in this war has commanded an armed merchant cruiser for 12 months, and has been a Commodore since 1941. As Commodore he has voyaged the equivalent of seven times round the world. He has been a fortunate man, for he has lost only seven ships with 16 lives. Considerable humour is in him, but there's bluntness, too. No doubt every Commodore has his idiosyncrasies, he says with a smile, and he's no exception. He speaks of the urgent need of keeping closed up. " I believe 10 per cent. of our losses are through straggling, sometimes only half a mile astern." He mentions fog, which they will probably run into, and explains that he will exercise sound signals in clear weather to get them accustomed to keeping station by sound. The convoy's good station-keeping depends largely on the Commodore's ship keeping her revolutions steady, he says, and he adds that he hopes his ship will behave herself.

He reverts to stragglers and says, now gravely : "I do try to nurse stragglers so far

CONVOY CONFERENCE. It is the last meeting before the convoy sails. Here final instructions are given on formation, dispersal, rendezvous, and all the intricate details of convoy tactics at sea. These men are Masters, each man is a ship, and each must know his place.

18

as I can, but there comes a time when it cannot be done. The safety of the convoy as a whole is the main thing". He emphasises that one of the main factors in safety is speed —" so I don't make emergency and evasive turns more than is absolutely necessary". He speaks of the time when clocks will be put back, which method he will use for signals, what a speed of so many knots will mean in fact, what to do if a ship is seen inadvertently showing a light. " I pray and beseech you to make a good black-out." He asks them not to break R.T. silence at night unless they have a " sitter". He speaks of the possibility of encountering ice and says, if that happens, a corvette patrol will be put out.

The D.E.M.S. Officer (Defensive Equipment Merchant Ships) then speaks, reminding them that sometimes they can use low-angle guns against torpedo or other bombers and their 4-inch gun against submarines on the surface. Some U-boats, he says, have been attacking at periscope depth in daylight, the periscope raised only for a few moments. If that happens, they should use their guns as pointers to help the escort, and similarly use tracer at night. As for " snowflakes", they will be told when to use them. An American captain remarks : " I have no snowflakes." D.E.M.S. Officer observes, smiling, that in that case he won't be able to use them, and the American captain joins in the laughter. The captain next says he would like a chance to try out his five-something gun—see if it works all right. He wanted to do it coming over, but they said he'd probably sink half a dozen ships if he did, and he laughs again.

The R.A.F. flight lieutenant now explains that if they do not always see the Coastal Command aircraft, it does not mean they are not there. He emphasises that smoke can be seen by aircraft 50 miles distant, and that air crews report that the smallest chink of light can be spotted : so both should be avoided. Aircraft approaching at night should not be fired at unless the ships'

crews are absolutely certain it is an enemy.

After another smile has been raised by a request that ships' officers and men wearing dentures should keep them in their mouths or their pockets, because men in open boats have suffered much from having left them behind, the Master of the convoy rescue ship —a small ship that sails at the rear—is asked to speak.

He is a Yorkshireman, who on one occasion saved 178 people in a convoy, and what he says is to the point. " When a ship is torpedoed, we must have some indication where it is, and which ship it is. If it is possible—I know sometimes it isn't—get a rocket or a wireless message away. That's what I would like." His ship, he says, has been fitted like a hospital—operating theatre, sick bay, etc. " The only thing the Admiralty don't do is to tell us how to get them out of the water. They say it is ordinary seaman's practice, but, believe me——" and he smiles drily, " it is *extraordinary* practice." He asks them to see that their lifejackets have their lights on and are in good order. The whistle, too. If it is blown continuously, the rescue ship gets a direction. Coloured sails in the boats are important, also ; it is almost impossible to see a grey boat on a grey sea. " Stay around your ship," he says, " no matter how long. If we have to steam over hundreds of square miles looking for you, it takes a long time, but wreckage helps us to find the place. If men on rafts or in boats can't help themselves when they get to our ship, my men will come over the side on to the rafts and boats to help you. They go over with a bowline all ready in a noose and before you know what is happening, you will be aboard." He explains two further points —first that his ship has scramble-nets attached to booms which are thrust out, nets which prevent men from drifting past, and to which they can cling ; and second, that ships' boats approaching his vessel should lower their masts. He ends, " Believe me, you won't be left". Voices murmur " Thank you".

Finally, the Senior Officer of Escort gets

up to say that a ship can be just as much a straggler ahead of the convoy, or abeam, as behind. He lends point to this by remarking that one night he saw a ship far ahead of the convoy and prepared to ram. " Imagine my horror when, just in time, I saw she was an enormous tanker ! "

This brings the conference to a close. The R.N. chairman requests them to hand in their confidential papers before leaving the meeting (they will be returned before sailing), informs them the times of boats to take them back to their ships, and concludes : " That's all, gentlemen. I hope you'll have a successful and pleasant journey".

The Masters gather in twos and threes greeting old friends, discussing their recent voyages and the prospects for this one.

At an earlier conference the latest information has been given of ships which have reached this port, or are coming, and whither all are bound. A chairman from the Ministry of War Transport presides over British and American naval officers, the army security officer, and a youthful W.R.N.S. officer. Through the window the sea is visible. A small pinnace dashes to and fro raising white water like a skier on snow ; the red paint on ships' hulls below the waterline catches the momentary sun. A flying boat passes across the sky.

As each ship is mentioned, a comment is made.

" She will come on the list to-night."

" Still waiting for tugs."

" Thirteen hundred twenty-three."

" She's Q.U. for orders."

" Haven't seen her through the boom."

" She's for the fast leg."

" Now at anchorage for 180."

" She's gas-freeing and goes up to-morrow."

" Returned owing to bad weather—she's U.C."

" She should have three operators because she's in the smoke party."

" She's to adjust to-day."

The list is gone through in time for one or

two officials to move on to the Masters' conference already described. Simultaneously, radio officers hold a separate conference, at which they are briefed before sailing.

There is a moment some hours before a convoy sails when the Royal Navy, in the person of the Commodore and his staff, go aboard a merchant ship. Here, throughout the voyage, the Commodore does his work of controlling the convoy in association with the Senior Officer of the Naval Escort. More than once the two have chanced to be father and son, for the Commodores (all ranking as Commodores, R.N.R.) are usually, although there are exceptions, men who had retired from the sea with the rank of Rear-Admiral or Captain, R.N., or were men who had commanded liners in our merchant fleets.

The Commodore takes with him a yeoman of signals, a leading signalman, three signal ratings and a Chief Petty Officer tele-graphist. The latter is usually a retired R.N. man, but the bulk of the signallers are " Hostilities only". A Commodore puts it thus : " After a short intensive course the signallers find themselves afloat, not knowing the back end from the stern. When introduced to my first yeoman, I asked him what he had done before the war. ' A signalman, sir', he replied. ' Splendid', I said, ' what ship were you in ? ' ' It wasn't a ship, sir,' he said, ' it was a railway box.' Of the remainder of my staff, one was a clerk in a county council, another a commercial traveller and a third a tea broker. Most of them thoroughly enjoy their present life and will find it hard to settle down again".

Whether the signalmen enjoy it (if " enjoy " is the precise word) more than the Com-modores is doubtful. A high sense of duty and a liking for responsibility, which find expression in treading a deck again—these give immense satisfaction kindling at times to a gaiety of spirit. One Commodore, after sailing the North Atlantic, asked for a voyage to Murmansk : he wanted some experience of being bombed, he said. And there is the

"HERE'S THE RENDEZVOUS." Master and Routeing Officer go over the charts together before sailing.

South of Ireland man of 56, just beginning his third year as Commodore, who showed alarm at the very notion of not continuing, arguing that he loves the work, can do nothing of equal service to the nation, and is fitter when he comes ashore than when the voyage begins.

The Commodores' average age to-day is 55 ; earlier in the war it was 60 and probably a little more ; one Commodore at that time was 68. The older men were usually of the Royal Navy ; the younger ones now taking over more of the work are often men from the R.N.R., some of them no more than 45 years old.

The task of looking after 50 or 60 or more ships is one of unceasing responsibility. The Commodore who takes off his clothes after the first night at sea is rare. " I some-times put pyjamas on and my clothes over them," said a Yorkshireman, " that makes you feel you've had a change. Personally, I can sleep anywhere at any time. When in Algiers last we were bombed two nights running, but I never heard the second lot—I slept through it in the chart-room " : the chart-room is on the top deck.

But at least one Commodore on the Murmansk run—it was a fairly quiet voyage as Russian convoys go—went to bed every night and had his bath next morning. Nothing perturbed him.

There are times when the hours are studded with signals received and given, signals by Aldis lamp to and from the naval escort and to ships in convoy ; signals by documents coming over by rocket fired from the naval escort. Decisions must be made whether to take evasive action and what sort ; and sometimes the hardest decision of all must be reached—whether or not to leave behind a straggler. One of our Commodores usually made a point of telling his convoy Masters : " I will never leave you behind, no matter how slow you are " ; but this is a policy that cannot always be maintained.

The Commodore's main problems lie, perhaps, in the heterogeneous nature of the convoy—this diversified assembly of ships new and old, oil burning and coal burning, of Masters with varying degrees of skill and experience, each with his own idiosyncrasies, Masters of several nationalities, whose readi-ness to follow, or ability to interpret, instruc-tions, is always unequal. Among the ships will be those with two or three knots " up their sleeve " who are tempted, in a crisis, to make use of them. Technically, a Master is responsible for his own navigation and if he decided to leave a convoy, could do so. Such an action is most rare. The Commodore's decisions, based on wisdom and experience, are usually accepted, and gladly.

The Commodore has his own trials arising from enemy attack and from foul weather. He was a man of wide knowledge who said he thought air attacks the more trying, but U-boats the greater menace. In a U-boat attack, he said, the night can be quiet until you hear a pop and you know one of your ships has been hit. As to weather, he had found the North Atlantic no pleasanter than the northern route to Russia. " In ice you're better loaded than light, for your Achilles' heel is the rudder and propellers—loaded, they're below the ice and safe from damage ; light, they may strike it."

Humour often breaks into the Commodore's relations with the Master in whose ship he sails, for the Royal Navy and the Merchant Service have many different customs "What time do we dine?" inquired a Commodore The Master replied they didn't dine.

What, then, did they have? pursued the Commodore.

" We have high tea", was the answer.

" And what time? "

" Five o'clock."

The Commodore pondered that. After a moment or two he inquired again, not without a sense of fun : "And what sort of entertainment can you offer me? " The Master replied that maybe the chief engineer would be willing to lend him his banjo.

There was the Commodore who, seeing one of the crew described on the documents as having been a barber, requested a shave at his hands. When it was done he complimented the seaman, who replied : " Thank you, sir. First time I've done a live 'un Used to shave corpses".

Those stories are told by the Commodores against themselves, and, indeed, are sometimes included in their reports. A Commodore has described how the ship's boy on the Russian convoy, being asked to make tea during an attack, made a brew of Edgeworth tobacco ; and another tells how he signalled a Master who had said that his supplies were running short, by reminding the Master of the miracle of the five barley loaves and two small fishes. To which the Master signalled back: " Yes, but I'm not the Almighty".

Good fortune in their work varies. A Commodore has sailed for over a year and voyaged to Russia without losing a ship in all that time ; a second has done the work for close on three years and lost one ship. A third has convoyed 1,500 ships and lost only three. Those men have been extremely fortunate. Luck is most capricious. Two Commodores have lost their lives on routes that are not regarded as highly dangerous, both having previously sailed the northern route to Russia.

Commodores seldom know whither they are bound till a day or two before convoy sails, nor do they know whether their quarters will be in a liner or in a tramp ship. They spend on an average some 125 days a year at sea. A good many Commodores—not fewer than 21—have gone down with their ships ; but the ranks do not diminish, and their spirit remains indomitable in spite of the rigours of their calling.

UP ANCHOR. Great chains slide over steaming winches, and the ships are released for the sea.

3. Equipment for Battle

WHEN our later convoys sailed to Malta, the merchantmen's own defensive barrage had become powerful. This steady growth in power is among the more remarkable evolutions in our convoys.

The right of the merchant vessel to defensive armament has been recognised for many centuries ; indeed, for about 700 years after England became a united nation, her fighting ships and merchant ships were virtually one. The last war showed the modern tendency. By September 1917, ships between 3,500 and 7,000 tons had two 4.7 guns ; over 7,000 tons they had two 6-inch guns and at a later stage depth charges.

The need for arming our merchantmen in this war therefore was foreseen. As long ago as 1937 Merchant Navy defence courses to train officers in gunnery and convoy work, and to teach seamen to be gunners, were begun at various commercial ports. These courses became more numerous nine months before war broke out. The stiffening of the merchant ship's fabric ready to take guns, the earmarking of pensioners and reservists—including a goodly number of Marines—for duty as key men to man the guns, the selection of officers and pensioners to work in ports on mounting the guns—all this was well advanced. What was not foreseen was the manner in which ships would become targets for air attack ; our preparations concerned themselves almost entirely with anti-submarine guns and paravanes.

The fitting of guns at home ports and ports abroad was started on the day war broke out. By the end of 1939, 1,500 guns had been mounted and the gunners embarked ; a year later ships carrying anti-submarine guns numbered 4,000. Stocks of 12-pounder guns were being converted for use as high-angle guns against aircraft, but they were not numerous, and until the spring of 1940 the only ack-ack guns on ships were a shuttle service of 120 Lewis guns, which moved up and down the East Coast, the guns being transferred from one convoy to another. Right up to the end of 1941 it remained a struggle to distribute the few short-range anti-aircraft guns to the best advantage. So desperate was the position that even light and sound rockets were issued at one period for firing at aircraft from ordinary Schermuly pistols. On one occasion an infuriated seaman hurled a Mills bomb at an aircraft flying very low, and hit it ; unfortunately, he had forgotten to take out the pin.

After the fall of France the manning situation was not easy, either. Volunteers, however, came forward, and to-day men serving in D.E.M.S. number 35,000—twenty-two thousand of them naval officers and gunners, and 13,000 sea-going Royal Maritime Regiment. In four years the expansion had been twentyfold. At the close of 1939 their numbers were only 1,696, all naval men. By December 1940 the figure had risen to 10,000, half of them soldiers at sea ; the year 1942 saw the previous total more than doubled. Early in 1939 there was a recruitment of catering stewards who had been robbed of their normal work, and were now turned into gunlayers. The first groups of ack-ack gunners were formed at Portsmouth in July 1940 from naval ratings not immediately wanted at sea. About that time, too, Army machine-gunners went to sea, taking their own guns with them ; these men defended vessels in harbour also—they were the nucleus of the Royal Maritime Regiment. Later, in 1940, " Hostilities Only " men who joined the Navy could be detailed for D.E.M.S. work and trained as seaman gunners ; that, too, is the method employed to-day.

By June 1943 the D.E.M.S. organisation had become world-wide ; it dealt with 7,000 ships, from large liners to the smallest tugs and fishing boats. Nowadays there are over

REHEARSAL. In port, a merchant sailor draws a bead on a model Ju.88 attached by wires to the mobile gunnery school.

50 bases for D.E.M.S. abroad and 46 at home.

Hardly any two ships are alike, so that the Merchant Navy has over 5,000 separate armament problems. Nor were ships designed to carry guns—rigging, derricks, rafts and a score of other things made gun-siting difficult. Top weight, balance and stability—these are always a worry. The weapons are an ordnance officer's delight (or is it despair ?) so varied are they—15 different types of low-angle and high-angle guns, six different sorts of machine-guns, and several kinds of rocket besides. There is the device called P.A.C., which throws up a wire many hundreds of feet. Not long ago the Master of a tramp ship called at a D.E.M.S. office to apologise. " It's about those P.A.C.s," he said : " You know, the instructions are to pull the darned string five seconds before the plane is overhead."

" Yes, that's about right."

" Well, I'm sorry, but in the excitement I pulled the string too soon—I reckon about one second too early."

" What happened ? "

" Well, the blighter saw the wire and dodged it."

" What a pity. What did he do ? How did he dodge it ? "

" Oh, he did the most wonderful aerobatics. It was a treat to see him. But he dodged the wire all right—it was most disappointing."

The Master, who had declined a seat, was now moving to the door. The D.E.M.S. officer said : " Never mind, when you're attacked next time, you'll pull the string a second later and you'll get him all right".

" Yes," said the Master with his hand on the door knob," " yes, maybe I will " (long pause). " You know, he fell upside down into the sea after those aerobatics ! "

Our merchant fleet has a long record of successes against the enemy. U-boats have been sunk by gunfire ; aircraft have been shot down into the sea and on to docks. Enemy airmen who have sometimes thought merchantmen " a piece of cake" have been powerfully disillusioned.

Our merchant and fishing vessels have by themselves shot down over a hundred aircraft, " probably " shot down fifty and damaged over a hundred others. Aircraft which the combined fire of H.M. ships and merchant ships have destroyed total well over a hundred more. But, of course, the merchantman's chief task is to bring her cargo safely to port. Fighting the enemy is incidental. If she goes into action, drives off the attackers, and arrives home, she has achieved her object.

In the beginning naval gunners handled only the anti-submarine guns, and soldiers the machine-guns and ack-ack guns, but the duties are becoming interchangeable. Moreover, it is not only the D.E.M.S. ratings who can handle guns and armament. The seamen themselves often take a gunnery course. Ten thousand are now qualified merchant seaman gunners, and 2,000 more are merchant machine-gunners. Apart from these fully trained men, over 100,000 men on our ships have taken a two-day course in the past two years, many repeating it at intervals. Training centres exist at all main ports, equipped with gun batteries, miniature tracer firing ranges, and lecture rooms. Buses have been fitted out with instructional gear and lecture rooms so that they can visit ships and give some training to men with only half an hour to spare. There are frequent shooting practices at sea, ships in convoy using parachute targets and smoke bursts.

The ships of our Allies are now defensively armed much as our own. The Norwegians have trained over 1,500 of their men for the work and the Dutch some 600. The Poles, Belgians, Greeks and Free French have trained men also ; if an Ally cannot find enough men, British ratings man the guns. The Americans have a complete organisation ; their ships often carry more armament than ours.

On British ships the normal equipment of a cargo vessel is an anti-submarine gun (usually 4-inch), a 12-pounder, and four or six Oerlikons. Troop transports and large liners have far more weapons.

One view of convoys and their defence is the Master's, or the Commodore's, or the Naval Escort's ; there is another from a stranger element. The pilot and crew of the Liberator, Halifax, Sunderland, Fortress, Wellington, Catalina, Hudson or Hampden that is seeking this company of ships to keep guard over them may find the sight of a convoy stirring to the heart and touched with beauty. Partly it is the relief at finding them and partly it is that at dawn or sunset the sea can be briefly tinted with pink or rose or gold and silver. With a scarf of mist lying on the horizon and this host of ships looking for the moment like a small township on the move—why, who can wonder that the airmen find it an invigorating sight ?

Our seamen for their part know well the assistance the aircraft give them, and many

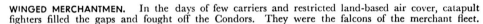

WINGED MERCHANTMEN. In the days of few carriers and restricted land-based air cover, catapult fighters filled the gaps and fought off the Condors. They were the falcons of the merchant fleet.

a man is inclined to cheer when he sees that this help from the heavens has arrived.

The first thing the captain of the aircraft and his men do on finding the convoy is to identify themselves as friendly. Then they begin to count the ships. They know how many there ought to be. Their eyes go up and down the lines spread over miles of sea—and usually two or three totals are arrived at. One lad says there are 48 ; another makes it 50. So once more it is done, till the number is agreed on. What relief if none is missing ! If there is, the Senior Naval Escort may signal with his Aldis lamp, " Have you seen the other part of the convoy ? " or " Will you go and look for our lame duck ? " And that is a thrill, too—to bring a straggler back to the fold.

The Master of such a straggler, a tanker, steaming slowly through a concentration of U-boats, was told he was 60 miles from the nearest convoy. He signalled to the aircraft, " Hell, have 5,000,000 gallons octane petrol aboard and could do with a spot of escort". He was given it by four Sunderlands, and as the last of them left him at nightfall he signalled his thanks. Another Coastal Command aircraft, after rounding up stragglers in a badly scattered convoy, received from the naval escort ship a signal : " Grand job, you're an angel".

What the air crew hopes for is the sight of a U-boat. After long searching of the seas—and probably out of view of the convoy, for close guard is not usually so profitable as the wider sweep—the white spume of a sub-

FLANKED BY THE ESCORT CARRIER'S ARM OF FIGHTER AIRCRAFT, OR COVERED BY THE LONG-RANGE

marine's bow-wave is observed. Down the aircraft dives to drop its depth charges. To avoid them a U-boat has been known to zigzag or even fight it out on the surface as five U-boats did which were destroyed by aircraft in 10 days in the North Atlantic in the spring of 1943. They first fired their guns when the aircraft were 1,000 yards or a mile distant. But more usually the submarine dives below—he can do that as fast as the aircraft can get into position to make its attack ; it is a question, first, which lookouts have the keener eyes, and next of wits and speed. A submarine was caught prowling along in a heavy sea towards a convoy six miles distant. The aircraft attacked it and simultaneously called up a corvette, which hurried to the fight and completed the work.

During March, April and May of 1943, when fights between aircraft and U-boats were numerous, 32 submarines were sighted from the air in a four-day battle, though some of them may have been seen more than once. On a rare occasion a Liberator captain came upon six U-boats within one hour and attacked three of them.

When an aircraft attack is successful, a patch of iridescent oil usually begins to spread over the sea, sometimes covering an area three-quarters of a mile long by a quarter of a mile wide.

But this does not mean that, if no U-boat is sighted, the aircraft's patrol is useless, or has not served its purpose. Submarines kept below the surface are submarines robbed of much of their striking power, deprived of

OF COASTAL COMMAND PATROLS, THE CONVOY MOVES STEADILY FORWARD UNDER A FLYING SHIELD

half or more than half their speed, and prevented to a considerable degree from shadowing a convoy with any ease. For all this, the seaman is profoundly thankful. He knows that, just as he himself has sleepless periods, the aircraft crews have sometimes spent up to 18 hours in the air following on many hours preparing for the flight, and that an aircraft captain has once or twice stayed with a convoy five hours over his allotted span because he was so vividly aware of the dangers that threatened the ships. It is not unknown for a navigator, on the aircraft's return to base, to fall fast asleep while his captain is being interrogated, and for the captain after his answers are given to fall asleep in turn. It has happened more than once that an aircraft captain on return to base has been unable to rest because he is obsessed by the predicament of the convoy he has left. He can still see in his mind's eye those darker shapes on the dark sea that were visible in moonlight up to eight miles away ; he still remembers the sight of them wallowing in the heavy seas, especially the tankers with the seas breaking over their low decks. If the night has been dark, the phosphorescence still runs before his eyes.

There is another piece of work for which seamen are grateful to aircraft—the discovering of survivors. On one occasion a pilot found six ships' boats tied together, looking to him on that broad ocean frailer than toys. The boats were in the midst of more than a mile of wreckage and oil. First he had seen crimson patches on the water resembling balls of stained wool ; these he had known for markers. His crew dropped a bottle of brandy and other emergency supplies, the bomb-aimer calling to the pilot: " Six hundred yards, five hundred ", till he got close by. Another pilot saw a white dot on the flat, green sea which proved to be the yellow sail of a boat. This was the end of a search in which aircraft had flown 25,000 miles in all. The air crew dropped a message which each had signed : " Ship will be with you 1750 hours. Best of luck and don't

worry. Drop us a line when you get back ". A third search ended with success after aircraft had flown in all 55,000 miles and spent 500 hours in the air.

We need not wonder that airmen and seamen feel warmly towards each other. To-day a scheme exists whereby a ship's Master can make flights and an airman can sail in convoy, that each may see at first hand the other's work and problems.

From the beginning of the war to the end of June 1944, Coastal Command aircraft have escorted over 6,000 ocean convoys—excluding naval convoys and single ships—and made over 1,500 attacks on U-boats.

The Royal Air Force's help is not the only help that comes from the skies. The Fleet Air Arm began to use the C.A.M. ship (Catapult Aircraft Merchantman) in the spring of 1941. The method was to catapult a fighter aircraft, often a Hurricane I, from a cargo ship, the aircraft flown by the Fleet Air Arm pilot. The first success in shooting down a Focke-Wulf was achieved on August 3rd, 1941, some 200 miles off Finisterre, after our pilot had been in the air nine minutes. Before that date, however, our pilots had frightened off enemy aircraft even though they had not shot them down. After a time Royal Air Force pilots joined the Fleet Air Arm in this catapult work ; both services endured the ordeal of crashing in the sea after the task was done, and both services had successes when guarding convoys to Russia, to Africa and Gibraltar or crossing the Atlantic.

Another plan was, however, taking shape. We had captured a German ship, the *Hanover*, employed in the banana trade. A flight deck was built on her, she was turned into a small aircraft carrier (immediately nicknamed by the Navy a " Woolworth carrier ") and given a new name, *Empire Audacity*. She went into service in September 1941, and Fleet Air Arm pilots flying from her deck American aircraft (the Martlet III, armed with .5 calibre guns) shot down several Focke-Wulfs within a few weeks. The enemy made very determined efforts to torpedo her and eventually succeeded—four torpedoes hit her—but not before she had herself taken an important part in the sinking of four or five U-boats, for her aircraft spotted for U-boats in addition to fighting off the Focke-Wulfs. Moreover, her work against aircraft, combined with that of the C.A.M. ships, had almost put an end to the activities of Focke-Wulfs in the Western approaches.

These small escort carriers have been used from that time onwards, sailing in convoy to America, to Russia, to the Mediterranean, and elsewhere. In a two-day air battle on the way to Murmansk in September 1942, Fleet Air Arm pilots shot down five torpedo bombers, probably shot down three others and damaged 14 more, for the loss of four of our Hurricanes, but only one pilot. Our men had flown through our convoy's barrage to get at the enemy. They have played a vital part in subduing the U-boats. Using Swordfish aircraft, the customary plan of action has been for the pilot to search for the U-boat and to depth-charge it; if the U-boat decides to fight on the surface, the Swordfish summons assistance and the carrier dispatches the improved Martlet armed with her cannon.

---

4. Men in Open Boats

In the spring of 1943 an able seaman named Henry E. Heinson, of London, was given the British Empire Medal for his spirit and resource in living for 18 days on a piece of wrecked ship still afloat; for food he had one cabbage and he eked out his jar of distilled water with snow, hailstones and rain collected by means of a canvas door. He

overcame monotony by propping up before him a photograph of his wife and talking to it; he massaged his feet and body three times a day, and he got what exercise he could by walking to and fro on his piece of wrecked ship. Both his body and spirit survived and he returned to his work at sea. About the same time a one-legged ship's captain named Donald Blyth was given the O.B.E. for his courage, after his ship was lost from torpedo attack, in leading eight men and swimming for eleven hours before being sighted by a seaplane which dropped two rubber dinghies.

These are two of the many awards for courage and endurance, given to men of the Merchant Navy who have survived shipwreck. Never in history, perhaps, has so much suffering been endured at sea after wreck; and never, fortunately, has progress in devising means to rescue life and reduce its sufferings been so swiftly made.

In the war's early stages, shipwrecked men often suffered agonies of thirst, exposure and frostbite. The enemy from time to time showed brutality in firing on ships' open boats and machine-gunning those swimming in the water.

Before this war it was uncommon for men to survive in open boats longer than 28 days. In this war, after 35 days in such boats, men have climbed to the deck of the rescuing ship without assistance, and after 37 days a man, in a well-provisioned boat, was so far from despairing that he could ironically ask his companions : " Is our journey really necessary?" It is on record that a Chinese was rescued after 130 days of exposure to the elements on a raft. If man's inhumanity to man has seldom reached such depths, man's tenacity in holding on to life has never been more clearly displayed. For men have sustained life on flying fish, or again have dived overboard and scraped the weeds from the boat's bottom, and attempted to derive a pitiful nourishment from chewing them. Imagination has played its part. In July 1941, when survivors from the *Saint Anselm* had been

18 days in their boat, a lascar appeared to be dying. No water remained and an engineer, thinking to make the man's end a little easier and happier, took some sea-water, mixed toothpaste with it and gave it to the man to drink. Within an hour he was able to sit up, and as all were picked up by a Spanish ship some hours later, he recovered. The makers of the toothpaste were asked if it contained any ingredient that would account for the lascar's recovery : they replied that it did not.

Men who have been torpedoed two or three times can be met with fairly often in convoy ports. A Master of 27 has been torpedoed six times, and at a Scottish port not long ago a chief steward 40 years old came ashore who was a survivor from his tenth torpedoing. He seemed normal. They are not always. A man came ashore at the same time who wanted to shoot the captain and first officer of the rescuing vessel that brought him in. He thought he was still in his own ship and that his own captain had been deprived of his post. Among the others was a seaman rescued for the third time and for the third time landed on this same quay. A fourth—he was a fat man—said he was alive only because he had lived on his fat : the others with him had perished. A fifth, the chief officer of a munitions ship, which blew up, said he remembered nothing of it : he came to in the sea with his arm round a bit of wreckage.

A man walked into a Government office in this port with nothing but shirt and trousers on. He proved to be a captain. First he had been for seven days in an open boat near Iceland, and then for 24 days in another such boat near North Africa. At Gibraltar he had volunteered to bring home a captured trawler and attempted to do so, but three days out from port she had sunk under him, sabotaged.

Bitter tragedy must inevitably form a part of the history of merchantmen at war. A survivor recently proved to be the only one living from a boatload of 53, many of them

LIFE AT THE EBB. Torpedoed, machine-gunned, suffering from shock and exposure, three sailors—two in the small boat and one flat out on the raft—sleep like dead men as they drift in the North Atlantic.

women and children. Again, a ship was torpedoed 400 miles from the Hebrides in May 1941. On the ninth day two died, one of them a boy who had drunk sea-water. Thenceforward, day by day until the eighteenth day, deaths occurred, sometimes one each day, sometimes three. Day by day bodies were committed to the deep. Yet again, when the *San Florentino* (Captain R. W. Davis) was torpedoed in the Atlantic in October 1941, the starboard midship boat which got away with 19 men was stove in, but floated deep in the sea on its buoyancy tanks, its gunwales under water. Sitting waist deep in that rough sea with a strong wind blowing, nine men perished in the 11 hours before the survivors were picked up.

These are but incidents in the long chapter of loss, a chapter starred with the names of famous ships, but starred also with heroism and sacrifice—as of the apprentice Donald O.

Clarke (posthumously awarded the George Cross), who was severely burned on legs, face and arms when the tanker in which he served was torpedoed, but disguised his suffering and laboured at an oar for two hours until he died, when his lacerated hands had to be cut away from the oar to release it. Fireman T. W. Blundell, of another torpedoed ship, suffering from a badly gashed hand, was on his way to a lifeboat when he heard a cry for help from the fourth engineer under a fiddley grating. Not knowing whether the ship was sinking rapidly or not, Blundell went hand over hand down the ash hoist, most of the ladders having been shattered, and extricated him.

Strange happenings are recorded. An officer kept a log written in minute hand on the back of labels from condensed milk tins. There was a boat from the *Clan Ogilvy* round which a whale 40 to 50 feet in length circled

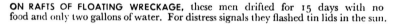

ON RAFTS OF FLOATING WRECKAGE, these men drifted for 15 days with no food and only two gallons of water. For distress signals they flashed tin lids in the sun.

several times. In a boat from another ship, they made cigarettes, using tobacco from a tin and, as paper, the love-letters which one man had carried carefully in his pocket ; as that vessel slid beneath the waves her siren began to blow and she vanished from sight with the siren still blowing defiantly. Water was dropped in a motor-car tyre by the South African Air Force to survivors on a beach, together with a note : " Will call again to-morrow. Love and kisses.--S.A.A.F."

And there is this note in a steamship company's report : " The rafts had drifted for 15 days during which seven of the men had died. Then a convoy was sighted and, on the bos'n's suggestion, a tobacco tin was tied to the end of a long-handled scoop to reflect the sun's rays and thus attract attention. Only one man had the strength to wave the pole, but by this means they were sighted. The bos'n, whose resourcefulness had been the means of their rescue, died 14 days later".

One wonders if Mr. Crusoe himself would have thought of the expedient that enabled a first mate sailing in an open boat near Nova Zembla to add to his food stocks. His ship had been sunk in Arctic waters and he made two landings on Nova Zembla to renew his water supply—this in the autumn of 1942. On his second landing he saw a large company of ducks on the rocks below him. He let down a line with a running bowline at the end. Promptly a duck placed its neck in the noose and was hauled up. In this way he caught and killed 140 ducks, and, making a fire, contrived to roast them, too.

Nor would imagination be likely to have invented the escape of Third Officer G. D. Todd and Able Seaman T. Clayton, when the *San Florentino*, mentioned above, was lost. She was struck by four torpedoes and finally broke in two, and the fore part slowly up-ended till it presented a grotesque sight, floating vertically in the Atlantic with the stem protruding 100 feet in the air. To this stem the two men had climbed, and they remained in that precarious position for 13

hours, sitting astride the bow 100 feet above the sea throughout a night on which a strong westerly wind was blowing and the sea was rough. When rescued they climbed 150 feet down the fore topmast stay. They had not eaten or drunk for 20 hours.

Men have shown an almost inconceivable power of endurance. Captain D. J. Williams, O.B.E., the Master of a motor vessel which had been sunk, wrote, on sighting land from his open boat : " So I got up. I had not slept night or day for 13 days. The weather and worry had kept me awake". Of the earlier days he wrote : " We continued on our passage, getting weaker each day, but still with determination. It was pitiful to see the men—in fact, all of us—when it rained, trying to catch water, all standing up with tongues and tins out to get the rain, and only catching a few drops". For 14 days he kept two life-boats together, and did not lose a man : 49 men were rescued.

The second officer of the *Empire Avocet* notes in his log of a similar journey : " I get them talking of past experiences, a thing which usually leads to friendly argument, so that they forget our circumstances for quite long periods. During the afternoon calms, when heat is intense, men have asked if they can go overboard. So far I had not allowed it for fear of sharks and because I thought salt on their lips might make their thirst worse. However, to-day I decided it was better to take risks than to have men going mad with thirst. It was organised so that there were never more than three in the water at once, while the rest kept a look-out for sharks". They reached a beach at length, rolled the boat over about 12 times, and set her bottom upmost with the stretchers under one gunwale, oars resting on the keel, and with the sail spread over them to make quite a serviceable hut. " By this time it was raining hard and seemed very cold. I lamented the fact that it was impossible to get a fire going. However, one of the firemen had been a ' swagman ' in Australia, and with the aid of a few scraps of paper from

Horlick's tablets and three or four dead twigs, he managed to start a flame. I sent parties to collect driftwood and we soon had a large fire going."

Nothing is certain when a ship is torpedoed. She may take hours to sink, or no more than minutes, according to her type, cargo and the damage done. Sometimes she does not sink at all. These extracts are from an account given by Mr. R. H. Wilson, chief engineer of a vessel sunk two degrees south of the Equator. The time was 4.30 a.m. " I was asleep at the time, but I was awakened by the crash and pressed the light switch.

Nothing happened. . . . I jumped out of bed and for a moment or two could not place myself. Everything seemed to be deathly quiet ; there was no vibration of the ship and no lights anywhere except for a few hand torches and I surmised she had been hit in the engine-room. I ran along the alleyway and opened the door. There was complete quietness down below except for the noise of rushing water." (He learned afterwards that both torpedoes had struck on the starboard side just aft of the midship accommodation.)

By the time he got on deck the deck aft

THE LAST HOLD ON LIFE. These men have been tossed for 10 days on storm-lashed seas. They have huddled together for some desperate comfort. Their arms are locked, their drenched limbs hug their upturned boat.

was practically awash. " I passed along the port side of the boat deck and there saw the chief officer trying to get the port aft boat away. It was very dark and there was a certain amount of confusion—quite unavoidable, I'm sure. Just as I was passing, I heard a kind of swishing sound. Looking round, I saw the boat hanging in a vertical position by the for'ard falls and a lot of men must have been spilled into the water."

He descended to the next deck and reached another boat, and as he did so the ship gave a lurch and a rope swung in towards him. He seized this and slid down into a boat, but a short while afterwards the vessel, which was going down by the stern, heeled over towards the boat. " I distinctly saw the funnel coming down towards me and decided it was time I got out of the boat—and did so. Almost instantly, it seemed to me, I was caught in the swirl and turmoil of the ship going down, but luckily I did not get entangled in any ropes. I have no idea how far I went under, but I swallowed a lot of water and my head and chest seemed to be bursting. Then I felt the pressure easing and my head came above water."

He clambered on to a raft on which, as dawn broke, he counted 16—three members of the ship's white crew, and three D.E.M.S. men, the remainder Malay seamen and Indian greasers. A vessel was seen making its way towards them and their hopes rose high, but it turned out to be a submarine and it stopped close alongside, asking various questions, among them—were there any officers on the raft ? " To this latter question I replied ' No.' I had taken off my lifebelt before he got too near, for it had ' Chief Engineer ' stencilled across it. He then circled round but later came close again, telling us there was another raft with a few survivors on it some distance away. I asked if there was a rescue ship in the vicinity. He answered he could not use his wireless but the first ' free ' ship he saw, he would give them our position. By ' free ' I presume he meant neutral. The commander was quite young— middle twenties I should think—and some of his crew congregated round the conning tower could not have been more than 16 or 17 years old. He asked us if we had plenty of ' pwowisions '—also if we would like some chocolate, cigarettes and a bottle of brandy. A tin containing the cigarettes and chocolate was then handed over, and a bottle of French cognac. The chocolate was also French. At the time these were being handed over, at least two of his crew were taking cine-camera pictures of us on the raft."

Three rafts were tied up in line astern of the big raft, and their occupants took stock of food and resources. They had 10 gallons of water in 2-gallon tins, and enough biscuits, sweet condensed milk, corned beef and meat and vegetable ration to last a long time. " Food wasn't our worry at all—just the water." The largest raft was about 12 feet long, 8 feet 4 inches across, and 3 feet deep. Down the centre was a trench 2 feet wide and 1 foot deep. At each end of this trench was a compartment holding a tin of water, a first-aid outfit, a tin of matches and a watertight container with distress flares in it. Under the floor boards was the biscuit tin and a box with tinned food, all the tins and first-aid outfits being coated with paraffin wax to keep water out and the tins from rusting.

Days were hot but nights cold and the dew heavy, and when day broke everybody was stiff and cold ; at that hour each man was served with a teaspoonful of cognac ; the bottle lasted three days. Following it, they had a piece of chocolate $1\frac{1}{8}$ inches long. Biscuits were available, if wanted. The first water ration was served at noon and the second and last before dusk, when a tin of corned beef was divided among the 17 men. Every third evening the ration was varied and a tin of meat and vegetable issued instead. " I had no great appetite for anything solid at all, except the chocolate."

A blanket had been brought to the raft from the ship and at night 11 men took it in turns to gain warmth from it. " Four

DEATH SHIP. For a month of days and nights this small boat has wandered in the Atlantic. It carries four survivors. They have watched twenty-four of their comrades die.

of us tried to sleep in the trench in the raft ; three others lay on paddles and bits of wood across the top of the trench ; and the remaining four occupied the sides of the raft. On the eighth day smoke was seen, but no more : the hull of the ship never rose over the horizon." That evening a turtle came in sight and got himself entangled between two rafts. The engineer and the bos'n managed to grip his flippers, flicked him on to the raft and turned him over. After discussing how to make use of him, they decided it was not possible and returned " a very startled turtle to his native element".

Day and night the rafts were surrounded by sharks of various species, varying from a yard in length to perhaps 9 feet. The larger ones were seen at daybreak and sunset. The men tried to catch a shark, having made

a hook from the wire handles of a water dipper and using a bit of cord for line. A few flying fish the size of sardines were usually found in the raft in the morning and these were used as bait. One morning as day was breaking the bos'n gave a yell ; there was a flurry and he dragged a shark aboard. The fish was gutted and one or two tried a bit of the raw meat, found it slightly salt but not too bad, so they decided to cut him up and boil him—in salt water, of course. The meat was cut up and placed in a chocolate tin, and a fire started by means of match-box labels, then pieces of the match-box itself. The meat when boiled was white and firm and many of the men appeared to enjoy it.

" There was no room for exercise and the only change we got from lying or sitting was to stand up and balance ourselves with a bit of wood." Some would swim from one raft to another ; others poured water over their bodies two or three times a day. Sunburn began to trouble them. " The left side of my face under the eye, the back of my neck, and legs and feet, were badly blistered and swollen. Feet were a problem. They felt so hot and burning all the time that my will power was not strong enough to resist the desire to keep them soaking in the sea and that made them worse by causing salt water blisters."

A small amount of time was passed playing draughts, for after the first tin of water was finished a draughts board was made by scraping the paint off alternate squares ; the draughtsmen were fashioned from the handles of distress flares made useless by salt water. They made wooden spoons from those handles, too. They kept count of the days by cutting a notch in a plank. It was on the twelfth day that a steamer's lights were seen. Three distress signals were set off, and the S O S was flashed on a hand torch. " As soon as we were quite sure he had seen us, we dished out a good ration of water to everybody—we had plenty to spare then." It was a Spanish ship which had changed its course from the Canaries to Cape Verde Islands owing to shortage of coal, otherwise they would not have crossed each other's paths. The ship—an old one and an ordinary merchant freighter—had hot sweet coffee and a kind of rusk biscuit waiting for them, and during six days on board they were treated with extreme kindness.

As early as September 30th, 1939, a British ship's Master and chief engineer (of the s.s. Clement) found themselves, their ship having been sunk off the Brazilian coast by the pocket battleship Admiral Scheer, aboard the German warship. They were among the first to be captured by raiders. Those raiders have included the Graf Spee and Scharnhorst, besides vessels masquerading as neutrals.

Over 4,000 merchant officers and seamen are prisoners, but a further number have been recaptured by our own warships (as on the occasion when the destroyer Cossack took on board 299 from the prison ship Altmark in a Norwegian fjord) or have made their escape by ingenuity and courage, sometimes leaping from moving trains when crossing Europe, and making their way home.

5. Rescue Coming

THE loss of 112 lives when the Athenia was sunk on the first day of war drew attention to the urgent need in war time for improving the means of saving life. Work to that end began at once.

From the day in December 1939 when a specification was issued by the Ministry of Shipping for a buoyant waistcoat to take the place of the standard lifejacket that was not suitable either for work or rest, to the present day when ships' boats and rafts are being fitted with water distillation apparatus, much thought, ingenuity and initiative have been used. Not only have Government officials charged with the task striven hard, but public-spirited scientists, members of both Houses of Parliament, shipowners, inventors, practical seamen and trade union officials have given willing help.

A civil servant engaged on the problems in the Ministry of War Transport developed the first type of small red light attached to a pocket battery which every seaman now wears on his buoyant waistcoat. Part, at least, of the idea sprang from seeing a bus conductor wearing something of the same sort when doing his work in the black-out. The civil servant found the firm who made similar lights and between them they evolved a clip-on device. This simple red light, which

THE SHIP OF HOPE. Hands wave in wild relief, faces turn up, as these survivors hear overhead the roar of the patrolling aircraft that will send their rescuers.

can be switched on and off at will (a necessary precaution at the time the enemy turned guns on those in the sea), has saved a host of lives—probably thousands. Another civil servant, colleague of the first-named, designed the protective suit issued to crews and passengers of merchant ships. This suit is windproof and waterproof and coloured bright yellow for wear in open boats and rafts, where it is equally effective as protection against extreme cold and a hot sun. It weighs 3 lb. 6 oz. and can be carried like a gas-mask. A third originated the idea of the simple wireless transmitter which enables a distress signal to be sent out automatically from a lifeboat.

These are but a few of numerous improvements. In oil tankers each member of the crew has flame-resisting garments with a protector hood, and each boat has a manual fire-pump and asbestos blankets. Every cargo ship must carry emergency rafts for everybody on board in addition to boats for all ; the raft is reversible—the bottom side is the same as the upper so that, whichever way it drops into the water, it can at once be used ; and it is manœuvrable like a boat. Moreover, every boat and raft has buoyant self-igniting electric lights which light up as soon as the raft reaches the sea. Passenger vessels, as distinct from troopships, must carry boats for all on board, and also buoyancy in the form of rafts and floating apparatus for everybody, so that each person is doubly provided for.

A further step was to require every foreign-going ship to carry a motor-lifeboat, capable of a voyage of 160 miles ; on oil tankers and ships carrying over 30 ordinary passengers two such boats are compulsory.

41

The rations were carefully considered. Chocolate containing a thirst quencher was added, together with malted-milk tablets and pemmican, commonly used by Arctic explorers. Biscuits were improved and the minimum water ration increased three times over. Shipowners usually add to the rations such articles as dried fruits, lime-juice, boiled sweets, and chewing gum, and provide boats with fishing tackle.

Sails in boats are now coloured a bright red, and a yellow or orange bunting flag is carried—these being the colours most easily observed. Smoke signals are provided in these colours also : they make an overhead cloud or long, slanting trail ; and there are hand rockets in the boats and rafts which fire five brilliant stars visible 10 to 15 miles off in good weather. A set of charts of the globe is placed in each boat and the compass is fitted with a luminous dial.

There have been improvements also in boat design. Especially noteworthy is the new type of steel lifeboat for tankers designed by the Tanker Tonnage Committee of the Petroleum Board in collaboration with the Ministry of War Transport. Before it was approved, the boat, with a volunteer crew, was tested in a static water tank and exposed for four or five minutes to intense fire and smoke. Water sprays—now fitted to all tanker lifeboats—were brought into operation and, though the flames reached at times a height of 40 feet, the seaworthiness of the boat was not affected and the occupants after their ordeal showed no signs of distress. Boats of this type, with minor modifications, are now in production. Half of them are powered by Diesel engines and the remainder by manual or electric means of propulsion. Another step forward in safety and comfort is a partly covered wooden boat for dry cargo ships, approved by the Ministry after passing severe tests of seaworthiness.

Among other improvements added in this war are skates fitted to boats so that they slide easily down the side of a listing ship,

better means of enabling people to cling to upturned boats, side-screens and canopies to shelter occupants of boats and rafts, first-aid outfits, blankets in waterproof coverings, folding ladders for men to get easily into a boat from the water, ingenious seat extensions to facilitate lying down in the boats, signalling mirrors, light fabric rain catchers with tubes to drain off the water to enable full advantage to be taken of rainfall, and items such as a whistle and lanyard, needle and twine, and oil for massage.

But far beyond most of these in importance

FIRST THEY WERE TORPEDOED. THEN THEIR R

is the design and fitting of an apparatus for distilling fresh water from the sea. A practical demonstration of what could be done was given by a chief engineer, Mr. Gordon Murray, adrift in the Atlantic with 23 men. He took the grave step of breaking up two oars to make fuel. By improvising a petrol tank as boiler, and burning the oars in a biscuit tin, he made a gallon of water on the first day of experiment. The Ministry of War Transport, the Admiralty and the Department of Scientific and Industrial Research, in collaboration with manufacturers, had

already carried out experiments, and to-day one of these distillers, using a patent solid fuel that can be saturated with sea water and still do its job, is being fitted as rapidly as possible in ships' boats. Production of a second design has started and a third is being considered.

It is, perhaps, not surprising that seamen have been heard to remark, with customary embellishments, that there's so much stuff carried in the boats now that you can't get in 'em yourself. This badinage hides a deep appreciation. Loss of life, suffering and

SHIP WAS BOMBED. THEN THEIR LIFEBOAT WAS MACHINE-GUNNED. FROM THIS RAFT THEY WERE SAVED

"WE ARE GOING MAD WITH EXCITEMENT". These are the sailcloth pages of a diary written by torpedoed men in their open boat as day by day they scanned the sea and sky for signs of rescue

hardship will continue, but they have been diminished. In recent months the loss of life on cargo ships sunk—the figure does not apply to tankers or passenger ships—has averaged 12 per cent. Of those who succeeded in getting into the boats and rafts from cargo ships, only $1\frac{1}{2}$ per cent. were lost.

Obviously the most effective way of saving life at sea is to keep damaged ships afloat. The outstanding success of this kind is the compressed air system, as applied by a former sea-going engineer for use in tankers. An air line is fitted the full length of the vessel and connected at either end to a compressor pump of the type generally used on the roads to power pneumatic drills. If the ship is torpedoed, air is pumped into the flooded compartments, driving the water out. Pressure can be maintained until the ship reaches port and repairs are put in hand. The Ministry adopted the system in June 1943, since when many scores of tankers have been so equipped.

Early in 1941 it was decided that the constitution of a deep-sea convoy should, wherever possible, and particularly on the more dangerous routes, include a rescue ship. Its business would be to sail at the tail end of the convoy and go to the aid of any ship that met with trouble, trouble being a comprehensive term. On the first voyage of the first ship devoted to this work, provision for survivors did not amount to much more than rows of mattresses put down between decks. To-day the ships are, so to speak, the R.A.M.C. of the convoy, and a convoy may easily comprise 2,000 people. The rescue ship carries a Surgeon-Lieutenant, R.N.V.R., two naval sick-bay attendants, and two naval signallers. The Commander and crew, about 60 of them, are merchant seamen.

In peace time these little ships of 1,500 tons or so rarely did voyages of over 40 hours' duration, and many no more than 16 hours'. They ran from the East Coast to the Continent—Leith to Hamburg, Hull to Rotterdam—or they did short journeys in the Levant with fruit and general cargo, or they

ploughed down from Glasgow to London. Nowadays they behave like leviathans, boldly sailing to Murmansk and Archangel, or across the North Atlantic, taking up to three weeks on the way. Several of the ships are 30 years old, and that is old for a ship. They are strongly built ; but some of them leak a trifle and most of them are uncomfortable, for they can roll—in the North Atlantic they can roll 40 degrees hour after hour and day after day, shipping a fair amount of water, so that a Surgeon-Lieutenant has more than once performed an operation with his feet standing in several inches of swirling sea.

The ships are now well fitted up with an operating theatre, sick-bay bunks with electric blankets, and beds for a large number (on one voyage a rescue ship saved 278 people). Each survivor is handed a kitbag as large as a small sack ; in it are a full suit of underclothing and ordinary clothing, together with boots and headgear. The ship carries 10,000 cigarettes, playing cards, games such as draughts and dominoes, and books and magazines.

It was a rescue ship's Master who said . " We don't look much more than a gadfly on the water, you know. We're not only rescue ship, but we're errand boy and charlady and God knows what, for we often pass messages from the Senior Naval Escort or the Commodore and we help to round up stragglers. One of our chaps once went down the line giving out the wireless news on his loud hailer".

The rescue ship's true work is done in the dark more often than not. She has two searchlights and sometimes she must use them if the work of mercy is to be done, though nobody is unaware how dangerous it is to use searchlights with U-boats in the offing.

When disaster occurs to a vessel in the convoy, the rescue ship makes her way to that vessel as well and as fast as she can. To sail diagonally across or through a convoy spread over miles of sea on a pitch-black night, or to find your way round it, to the ship that has been struck—even a landsman must have some small notion of what this means. A storm may be raging at the time. The small ship threads her way along, dodging the bluff, massive tramps and the tankers shipping seas across their low free-boards, getting her rescue tackle ready. She has two great baskets on deck, as high as a man, and five feet across the top. These go overside on a derrick with a seaman inside, and this seaman fishes for men. In the same way booms are thrust outward, from which scramble-nets hang down five feet below the surface, and thus the ship trawls for men.

"The only safe assumption", say the men who do the work, "is that the survivors will be unable to help themselves. Once within sight of rescue, they often seem to collapse." It can be a fearful job getting them aboard, partly because they are numb with cold and partly because they are so heavy, their clothing saturated with water. Some of the ships have fixed up a snatch block and tackle for hauling men up ; without it, you may need half a dozen men manhandling a line to bring a survivor up the ship's side.

It has become more or less routine for seamen to go overside to help, to go down the scramble-nets till they are waist deep in the sea. Firemen go too—it is difficult to keep firemen below decks when the rescue work is on ; and the chief engineer will say up the speaking tube to the Master : "If you'd like to change places, that's O.K. by me. How many visitors have we got up to now ?" Meanwhile, rafts bearing survivors may be rising and falling on tumultuous seas, and rescuers will have climbed down to them with bowlines to place round exhausted men.

When a United States tanker was tor-pedoed in November 1942, a British able seaman at work rescuing the American captain was himself dragged into the sea several times before he could make the bowline fast. Again, it is recorded by a Master in February 1943 : "Two sailors went down on the raft in bare feet to secure lines to survivors. The seas were estimated

at about 30 feet. One raft was on the weather side. Only when the last man was lifted on board did they themselves return. The great majority of the crew, including engineer officers off duty, firemen and stewards, eagerly helped in some way, such as stripping off clothing and rubbing down with towels". It is playfully told how a certain mate, who suffered from the delusion that his ship harboured an "Anti-Mate League", went overboard to help, and how his suspicions were deepened when, on being helped back overside, he was somehow or other dropped back into the sea. This note on a sick-bay attendant is dated November 1942 : "Under the most trying circum-stances he ministered to the sick and injured and for three days and nights denied himself any sleep".

Officers of these ships have occasionally been without rest for six days. A Master remarked : "I wedge this armchair between the bookcase and the wall and I sleep in it, with one ear cocked. But you get that way you can't sleep a long time, anyhow ; I've seen it take three days in port before I got a good night's sleep".

Another glimpse of the work is given by a Master's letter written in the winter of 1942-3 : "Let your imagination dwell on a real dirty night in the Atlantic with a heavy sea running and pitch blackness enclosing you. Suddenly the scene is changed : explosions, the result of attack, and the whole area lit up by Snowflake rockets. Merchant ships scattering. A weird and uncanny sight. We wheel out of the convoy and head for the scene of operations. What the thoughts of my officers and men are, I don't ask. A job of work has to be done and right well they do it. After seven hours' work we head off at full speed to rejoin the convoy, an extra 80 lives on board". He adds laconically : "A further alarm came during dense fog·

RESCUE IS HERE. Hands reach down to draw them out of the sea. A solid ship awaits them, with food and drink, dry clothes, and a place to sleep·

Gunfire was heard and flashes seen on the starboard bow. Speed was reduced and course altered in the direction of the gunfire. A searching sweep was executed. A submarine was reported four points on my starboard bow by two look-outs. Course was immediately altered in that direction and speed increased to full".

Some further enlightenment comes from a Master whose ship had just picked up 256 survivors : " In addition to picking up survivors there was very heavy signalling work to attend to on the bridge, and from November 1st to November 7th my officers were practically without rest, as were the three radio officers. I snatched such sleep as I could alongside the helmsman on the wheelhouse deck. . . . We had great difficulty in breaking out of the ring of submarines surrounding the convoy. . . . On November 3rd, the ship was badly shaken by a most violent explosion underneath it . . . several other ships thought they had been torpedoed . . . as far as I could gather it was felt equally severely all over the convoy . . . it was far worse than either torpedo or depth charge" .

To ensure that nobody is left behind, a Master will sometimes sweep when daylight comes an area of 50 square miles, crossing it at angles or sailing round in circles that he and his look-outs may so far as humanly possible scan every piece of it. When day has broken, a ship's boat may be seen two or three miles off, and much farther if she carries a red or yellow sail ; a raft may be hard to discern at more than half a mile. Nothing is certain ; the sea that is running and the degree of visibility count for much. As for the night that is moonless with low rain-cloud—a night when a blacked-out ship can be wellnigh invisible 100 feet away—then nothing but the light on a boat or raft will help them find it, and that light may be one that moves as though bewitched, one instant poised on a high wave and the next vanished in the gulf. When the rescue ship nears the survivors, she must usually stop her engines and drift—drift in order to be slow enough in approach—and she will probably do it pretty well beam on, keeping the wind four or five points on the quarter. One night, such a ship had to drift down in a heavy sea, rolling her 40 degrees, with a hole in her hatch open to any water coming that way, for just before the survivors were lighted on, a raft had broken loose in the ship's rigging and stove the hatch in. It was a more ticklish job picking up nine men at that moment than a hundred on another occasion, but it was done.

Many a rescue ship has sailed 2,000 miles and more and, happily, had no work to do ; but more than 3,500 people have been saved from the sea by these ships, among them wives of Russian diplomats and a number of children, a Commodore of convoy, and officers and seamen of all the Allied Nations. On one occasion a rescue ship was herself torpedoed, but a second rescue ship in the same convoy (seldom do two sail together) saved all her crew but one.

Some survivors growl from the moment they get on board : " they want bacon and eggs for breakfast", as a Master put it ; nothing is right. This attitude is one form of reaction to their ordeal. More commonly it takes the shape of profound gratitude and a desire to make gifts. Again, a man having once survived may face ensuing perils with a measure of equanimity, knowing a torpedo is not necessarily the end ; but another man may be doubly apprehensive and be drawn at night to the boat deck where he feels safer. The sick-bay attendants are familiar with what can be expected, neither losing their tempers with the disgruntled nor encouraging gratitude in the rest ; they have the same genius as Mr. Atkins for taking things as they come, and persuading with little or no foreign language half a dozen races to do what is required of them. As for the Surgeon-Lieutenants, they have tackled most problems up to appendicitis, and even a case of trepanning.

SHIPPING : THE PLAN AND ACHIEVEMENT

6 The Course of the

Battle

BEFORE attempting to describe the organisation of shipping in this war, the development of convoys, and the work of the major convoy routes, it may be well to note the phases into which the war has fallen from a shipping point of view. Looked at broadly, they number five, the first ending with the fall of France, and the fifth beginning with our landings in North Africa, and stretching into the future.

Up to June 1940 shipping was mainly concentrated on bringing food and materials into Britain and France, and on moving men, weapons and supplies over short distances into Western Europe. The first British Expeditionary Force was transported to France on a pre-war plan and almost without incident—a strange beginning to total war. Perhaps the outstanding fact was that the B.E.F. was transported and maintained for close on nine months with the loss of only

one ship, and that loss not due to enemy action.

From the English Channel and Bristol Channel ports we shipped our troops and supplies to Cherbourg, Brest, St. Nazaire and Nantes ; to Caen went mainly petrol, ammunition and stores. In November we began to employ train ferries from Harwich and Dover to take excavators, ambulance trains, and heavy and light locomotives of which we transported 110. By the end we had sent to France 60,000 vehicles. The ships used were all British. In the first 27 days we transported 157,000 men, and in the first 50 days 24,000 vehicles. From January 1st, 1940, to February 5th, 1940, we took across a further 84,000 men, and reinforcements continued to flow, from time to time, until June.

Convoys were begun in this period, the first leaving British ports on September 7th, 1939. Among the more notable and most trying of the early war voyages were those to Narvik for ore, at first unescorted and next in convoy—voyages troubled by foul weather and icebergs so that they were to this extent a foretaste of Russian convoys. In the first phase, the earliest guns were placed on board merchant ships. Another important step was

49

THE PHASES OF THE SEA WAR

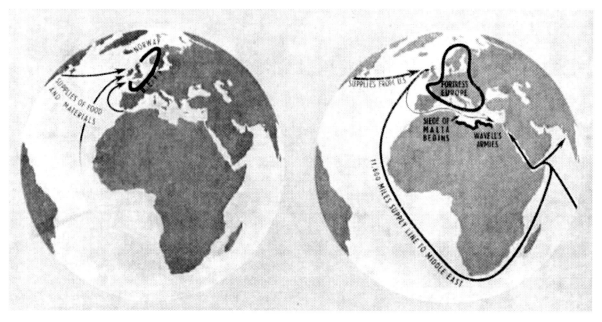

1. In Close Waters: SEPT. 1939—JUNE 1940

2. Long Haul: JUNE 1940—JUNE 1941

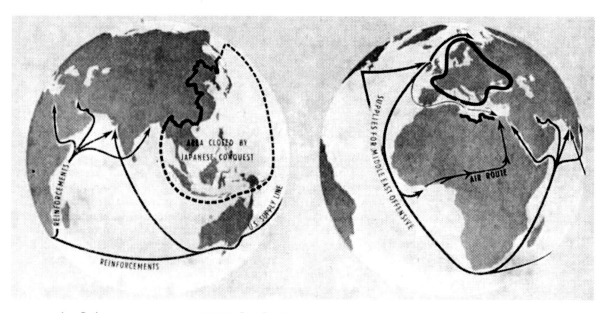

4. Defence against Japan; Middle East Build-up: DEC. 1941—OCT. 1942

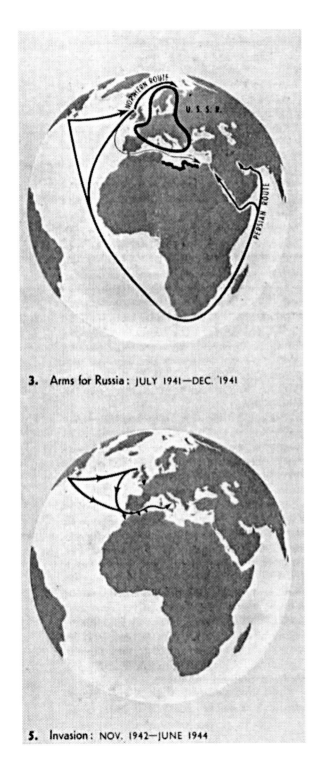

3. Arms for Russia: JULY 1941—DEC. 1941

5. Invasion: NOV. 1942—JUNE 1944

the control of the ships themselves—slowly but firmly assumed. In October and November 1939, for example, tonnage was requisitioned for carrying cereals from North America, and the policy of time chartering foreign ships was launched. Early in 1940 the Anglo-French Shipping Executive was set up and by the spring of that year ambitious work was being done by the Anglo-French Co-ordinating Committee towards joint programmes. Large amounts of shipping tonnage were devoted to coal for France.

The war was only a few weeks old when our ships began to be sunk by magnetic mines. Between November 18th and 22nd, 15 ships were lost in this way. We countered with degaussing. Although fitting this apparatus caused inevitable delays to sailings (at one time we were using 1,200 miles of wire cable a week on this work) the results were admirable ; for instance, the world's biggest liner, the *Queen Elizabeth*, was enabled to sail on her maiden voyage to New York. A device which some ships' crews had looked on as a " Christmas tree of wire " became a defence they soon regarded as vital.

In this phase the *Graf Spee* and other surface raiders began their attacks and the spectacular episode of the *Altmark* occurred. The U-boats had not yet appeared in great strength (the enemy seemed to be pinning his major faith to mines) and although our shipping losses during the war's first week or two were heavy, they averaged up to the fall of France no more than 100,000 gross tons a month—serious but by no means crippling.

This period was the only one during which we had full use of the short sea routes to west and north Europe ; in the spring of 1940 the invasion of Norway lost us many short-haul sources of supply. Not till Dunkirk did the English Channel begin to be largely closed to shipping. Till then great vessels ended mighty voyages in London docks.

Of the evacuation from Dunkirk no description is given here, because the Merchant Navy's part in that task will be described in a companion book on our coastal shipping. Good work was done also in bringing soldiers of other nationalities and civilian refugees to this country from ports in the Mediterranean or the neighbourhood of Brest after the collapse of France.

On Italy's entry into the war in June, another sea, the Mediterranean, became partially closed. The credit side of phase number one holds the acquisition of Norwegian, Danish and Dutch shipping. This eased the position, although not for long.

Phase number two covered a year—the year when Britain stood alone against the enemy, save for the gallant fight put up by Greece against Italy and the vital help in supplies given by the United States. It was the period of what can be called " the long haul", for the near sources of supply were lost and stringency of exchange added its own problems. Simultaneously, the fall of France robbed our sea routes of many naval escort ships, so that difficulties grew rapidly.

It was during the first three months of phase two that we developed the 12,000-mile route by the Cape to the Middle East, and it was two months later—in October 1940—that Italy attacked Greece and we grappled with our first problem of supplying a distant ally, sending her well over 100,000 tons a month. Ports and communications in the Middle East area were vigorously improved, but early in 1941 the passage of convoys through the Mediterranean became more and more difficult, and the Siege of Malta began. In March our armed forces landed in Crete and Greece, and both in supplying them and eventually withdrawing them we suffered shipping losses. At home, our ports underwent heavy bombing.

Our problems were many and serious, and we made many attempts to solve or ease them. A campaign for quicker turn-round of ships was begun ; a Middle East Supply Centre was established to develop and distribute the area's own resources ; our importing programmes were rigorously cut down and tightened up so that a greater

austerity made its appearance in British life. More important than these was the growing help from America. Our first contracts for building ships in the United States were placed in December 1940 ; in the following March was passed the Lend-Lease Act, and in May the United States placed some of her ships at our disposal for voyages to the Red Sea, the Persian Gulf and India. She also began to patrol the Atlantic, adding her patrols to ours.

The third phase covers the second half of 1941, and runs from the invasion of Russia to Pearl Harbour. The first of our Russian convoys were sailed by the Northern route. The Japanese occupied Indo-China and we gave active help to our Chinese ally by the Burma Road. We, together with our Russian allies, occupied Persia and began the development of the Persian route to Russia—a route to be used so extensively at a later stage by the United States. In Russia the Moscow Protocol was signed and the Anglo-Soviet Shipping Committee was set up—the first official Anglo-Russian body with joint responsibilities to function since the Russian Revolution.

Shipping during this phase was immensely complicated by reason of new and prospective theatres of war and because America's part was still fettered by the Neutrality Act. Our shipment of military cargoes was growing swiftly throughout.

Phase four runs from December 1941 to November 1942—the year which began with Pearl Harbour and ended with British and American landings in North Africa. For the man who was handling ships it was a period of frequent changes in the demands made on tonnage, and of shipping diversions to meet a situation which never remained static. We lost sources of supply in Malaya, Burma, and the Dutch East Indies ; and we assigned to Australia, which was gravely threatened, additional tonnage to carry the necessary materials and men.

British merchantmen were in both Singapore and Rangoon until the last. Ships hung on with great determination in Singapore to bring away cargoes of precious rubber, and a score of cargo vessels and four or five of our troopships landed a division of troops a brief while before Singapore fell. Not all those ships withdrew safely. Merchantmen sailed from Singapore carrying as many as 2,000 refugees, some of them occupying the ships' holds.

At Rangoon, four cargo vessels remained until the demolitions were blown and 300,000 tons of oil deliberately fired on March 7th, 1942. Merchant seamen were there, as they were in most other Far East ports up to the moment of evacuation.

The creation of an Anglo-American Combined Shipping Board was a new step of enormous value. When we lost Tobruk, America at once sent fast ships with Sherman tanks direct to the Red Sea. Meanwhile, we were developing the West African route to the Middle East, unshipping and assembling aircraft on the West Coast and flying them overland. The fourth phase was one of strain and anxiety, relieved in Britain by a fine harvest, and lightened at the close by the Eighth Army's triumph at El Alamein, by the promise of the North African landings, and by the fact that output of new ships in Britain and America had begun to overtake losses.

The fifth phase, which began with the new North African campaign, included the landings in Sicily, Italy and Northern France and is not yet closed, saw the Merchant Navy taking ships of assault right up to hostile coasts and fortifications—a task that was to some extent new to them. They had been in the front line at sea from the start ; this was front line work of a different sort, or at least on a grander scale. Encouraging signs appeared —foremost among them our growing ability to keep the U-boat packs at sea under control and to sink them at a faster rate. The Atlantic lifeline gained both strength and security. Joined to this success was the increasing margin of shipbuilding over losses and a recovery in imports to Britain.

7. The Strategy of Shipping

BEFORE a deep-sea convoy can sail, a good deal of organisation is needed. To move a vessel across the world is a complicated piece of work at the best of times. Crew, bunkers of coal or oil, water, the cargoes she will carry, the route she will take, the repairs she may require abroad—these demand forethought. Weather may be bad, seas treacherous. All this in peace. During war the problems are multiplied a dozen times, for if moving one ship is a complex task, what of a convoy of 20 or of 80 ships, and a score of such convoys ? Nothing but a central control has enabled it to be done.

This control rests in the Ministry of War Transport and it is exerted with one fixed purpose—to make sure that every ship carries to and fro on our business every ton she can, or in a more technical phrase, that not a ton of carrying capacity is wasted.

Each time a department of the Ministry allocates tonnage for this or that purpose, fixes a loading area, or shifts a programme of imports or exports, the purpose is the same—economy. That is true even of the work of Sea Transport Division, which is an integral part of our fighting machine and handles many problems, from the movement of troops and military equipment down to the provision of ships for distilling water.

Our life and the sea are joined ; without the sea we cannot survive. That is why the Atlantic route has rightly been called our lifeline. Moreover, ships are a root problem, if not the fundamental problem, in every operation. Our invasion of Europe could not begin till the Mediterranean was opened, and a principal reason for opening that sea was to save ships and tonnage, since one ship direct to Suez can do the work of two sailing via the Cape.

HIGH COMMAND. Ships must be routed, ships must be defended. On the great wall map, left, a WAAF plots the course of protecting aircraft along the bright latticework of their patrol lines. Above is the operations room of Western Approaches. In the Ministry of War Transport chart room, below, the movement of every British merchant ship is plotted and recorded.

It hardly needs saying, then, that our ships and their carrying capacity stand very high among the assets on our balance sheet. How to guard them, how to increase their numbers, how to use them with the greatest skill, how to avoid waste of every sort—these have been, and remain, our problems.

This is as plain to our enemies as to us. Both in the last war and in this, Germany has striven to reduce our ships to a number and capacity on which we could neither fight nor live. For many long months in this war, a main preoccupation was to meet essential needs with a fleet of merchantmen steadily shrinking owing to destruction by war at sea. To-day the building of new ships exceeds sinkings; we have ground for believing the worst is over, for new tonnage is now available for our offensives.

We have economised in shipping in several ways. First, we stopped importing that which was not essential to our life and the war effort. "Everything vital but nothing not vital" was the rule. Next, we planned to shorten routes by gathering imports from the nearest source, or from sources which fitted routes best. Third, we began to save weight and space in food imports. One of the first moves was to eliminate fresh fruit almost entirely and concentrate on meat. At the beginning of 1941 we began to take the bone out of meat and the shell and 90 per cent. of the water from eggs. Beef now goes into three-fourths of the former space and some of it (made up into square blocks) into two-thirds of the space. Eggs no longer require refrigerator ships to bring them across the seas, and in big ships carrying beef and mutton we now save nearly 100 voyages a year. No man can be expected to read with pleasure of dehydrated meat that looks like sawdust; but perhaps he will be pacified by knowing that it takes only one-third of the room in a ship's hold and that not refrigerated.

Other vital economies have been made by improving methods of packing and stowing. How can you best fill the awkward corners left in a ship's hold when tanks are loaded? Which vehicles can be stacked one on top of another? (Jeeps are among the few.) What can you compress, divide or take to pieces? Much has been accomplished here. Lorries, guns and aircraft usually travel in cases, after dismantling. Awkward projections are removed.

This task of achieving economy in ships, begun in London, is continued at ports both at home and abroad. Port Directors, Port Emergency Committees, Sea Transport Officers (many of them retired sea captains), marine surveyors and Mercantile Marine Office Superintendents, work in close association with Admiralty Flag Officers and staffs, dock authorities and shipping companies, various trade unions of officers and men, and the Shipping Federation which operates "The Pool" of merchant seamen. All are alike intent on making the best use of our ships, and turning them round in the shortest time, for every day or hour saved in port increases the tonnage available. A problem typical of those that arise may be mentioned here: whether to bunker for both out and home on certain voyages, and thus avoid sending colliers or tankers to replenish intermediate bunkering stations. Double bunkers mean so much the less cargo carried. Is the saving in colliers and tankers worth that loss? A nice point.

Feeding and supplying the United Nations —which means a large part of the whole world—has been possible only by pooling Allied shipping. To-day there are two pools, one controlled by the Ministry of War Transport, the other by the War Shipping Administration of the United States. Every United Nations ship goes into one or other of those pools. To co-ordinate those controls two Combined Shipping Adjustment Boards exist: one consists of Lord Leathers and Mr. Philip Reed, who succeeded Mr. Averil Harriman in London, and the other of Admiral Land and the Hon. J. S. Maclay, who succeeded Sir Arthur Salter in Washington. The American pool helps us with supplies to the United Kingdom, Middle East, etc., and we on our part provide shipping assistance to the U.S. wherever we can.

A complete record of ships in the British pool is kept in the appropriate Ministry division ; and when ships are needed for a particular task, whether military or civil, they are chosen not by nationality but by suitability for the task, and according to where they are at the time. A " taxi-rank " of ships, so to speak, is always kept for emergencies ; but not even new convoys, such as those to North Africa, Sicily and France—the greatest sea expeditions the world has yet known—could be allowed to put a stop to the other great routes across the Atlantic, to the Middle East and so on. It will be understood why men controlling our ships work with some precision six months ahead—our chief imports are planned 12 months ahead—and try to work 18 months ahead. A sudden demand can be equivalent to throwing a large boulder into the shipping pool.

The foregoing is but the barest outline, as perhaps an illustration will show. The Ministry of War Transport has a chart room of which the old phrase " seeing at a glance " can be used. One wall bears two charts each some 20 feet by 10—maps of the world showing the disposition of our ships. One chart is for British ships only, the other for foreign vessels. One can see in a flash where the ships are (for each is represented by a small coloured flag or button), how they are clustered in particular ports, how many convoys are at sea, and where those convoys are. Each flag or button is numbered and coloured according to nationality and type of ship, and the card index in the same room tells the history of that ship since the war started. Day by day cables in code arrive from Admiralty and other officials spread throughout the world, and girl clerks bring the card index up to date and revise the charts. In addition to the wall charts are one or two table charts—one a coaling chart for the Middle and Far East.

Merchant Navy is a title so firmly established and so honourable that many a man, no doubt, has been led to suppose that it is as closely knit and organised a body of ships and men as the Royal Navy and on a command, like the Navy, moves into action. Yet from the nineteenth century onwards the two forces have become well defined and distinct from each other, and, while a large number of officers and men of the Mercantile Marine belong to the Royal Naval Reserve and move into the Navy as soon as war breaks out, the bulk of its men and ships, in a war's initial stages at all events, continue their work much as they do in peace. Our merchant ships are not the State's ; they are privately owned. For example, when this book was planned, nearly 300 shipping companies were asked to submit suitable records of what their men and ships have accomplished in this war. It is only war which draws the " fiery particles " of the Merchant Service together, from the *Queen Elizabeth* to the coasting collier, and welds them into a unity ; that unity is controlled by the Ministry of War Transport. Moreover, the situation is rather more complicated even than this, for about one-third of the total tonnage in our service is foreign. At one time, for instance, probably 40 per cent. of the oil brought across the North Atlantic came in Norwegian tankers, and there are ships serving the United Nations' cause which fly the flags of Belgium, Greece, Holland, Poland, Russia, Yugoslavia and Free France, besides the enormous fleets of America. In addition, vessels belonging to Sweden, Denmark, Latvia and Esthonia are working for us.

The requisitioning of ships by the British Government began early in this war—tramp ships by December 1939, and all liners early in 1940. Tramps are ships which in normal times have no fixed route, but call at various ports to lift cheap and handy bulk commodities such as grain, coal, ore, timber, scrap or phosphates. One of their first big tasks in this war was to carry bulk cereals across the Atlantic. Others were taking the

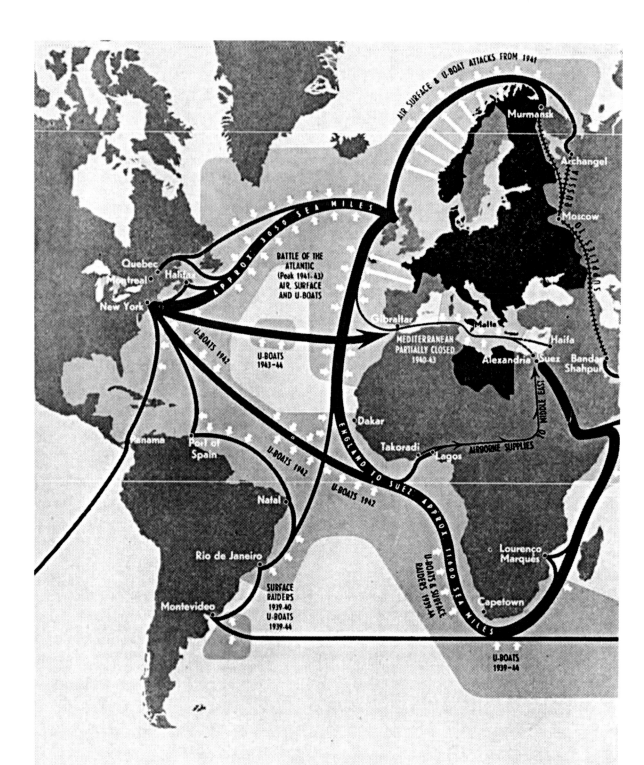

THE ROUTES AND THE RISKS

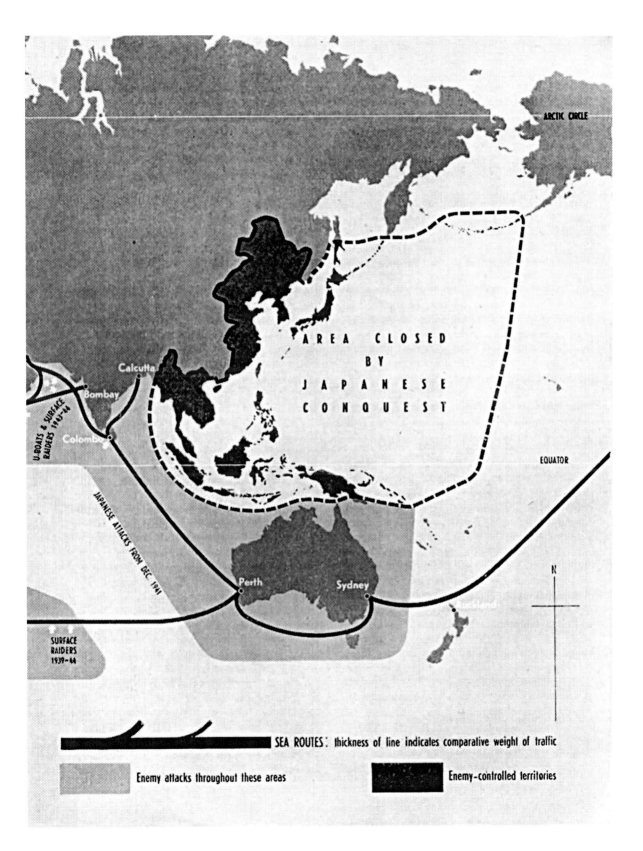

ARCTIC CIRCLE

A R E A   C L O S E D
B Y
J A P A N E S E
C O N Q U E S T

Calcutta

Bombay

U-BOATS & SURFACE RAIDERS 1942-44

Colombo

JAPANESE ATTACKS FROM DEC 1941

EQUATOR

Perth

Sydney

N

SURFACE
RAIDERS
1939-44

SEA ROUTES : thickness of line indicates comparative weight of traffic

Enemy attacks throughout these areas

Enemy-controlled territories

first B.E.F. to France and bringing ore from Spain To-day they take out military cargo to theatres of war and bring back supplies of all kinds A tramp owner has been known to point out that his ships are now merging into White Ensign ships judging by the way they are shelled, bombed and torpedoed.

The word "liner", as used in the trade, means a cargo-liner which may or may not carry a few passengers. She takes a mixed cargo, usually has two or three decks to facilitate stowage and loading, and sails to fixed places at a speed up to 15 knots or so. She is often five or six knots faster than the tramp ship and 5,000 tons deadweight heavier—that is to say, she is up to 15,000 tons deadweight. It is the tramp ship, in the main, which has sailed on the convoys to Russia, and it is the cargo liner that has done the chief work to Malta. A number of tankers, of course, have sailed on each route. Like the sturdy tramps, cargo liners have been in the front line throughout. Greece, Crete and the Eastern Mediterranean—all these have been well served by them, notably by the fast refrigerator ships.

But although British ships are under Government control (a charter fixes financial and other agreements), the shipowner still acts as ship's husband, providing crew, bunkers and stores, and looks to repairs and general fitness. It is true that the creation of " The Pool " of officers and men, administered by the Shipping Federation to ensure a constant supply and thus prevent a ship being held up for men, has wrought immense changes ; but many companies keep the officers, engineers, bos'ns and carpenters they had in peace time ; loyalty is deep on both sides. One further point—as new ships are built they are allotted to shipowners for management, to replace those which belonged to them and have been sunk or destroyed on the seas in this war.

Although this book is a record only of ships and men sailing under the Red Ensign, tribute can be paid here to the fine and invaluable work done by Allied ships, and a note made of how those ships, other than American, are controlled.

When Norway was invaded it became imperative to take action over Norwegian ships A night or two later a meeting was held in London attended by Mr Colban, the Norwegian Minister, Mr. Robert Hudson, then our Minister of Shipping, and Mr. Hysing-Olsen, a leading Norwegian ship-owner, who had been on his way from London to Norway when invasion occurred and had at once flown back At this meeting, which did not break up till 2 a.m., Mr. Hudson announced that the British Government, to ease the situation, would take over the insurance of all Norwegian ships. A message was drafted for Norwegian ships and transmitted to them by the Admiralty wherever they were, instructing them not to return to Norway or to enter enemy or neutral ports. In addition, the B.B.C. broadcast messages to them " at dictation speed". Although the enemy forced Norwegians at pistol point to speak at the microphone in Oslo declaring the London messages bogus, that had no effect. Not a single Norwegian ship failed to obey the London request, backed as it was by the Norwegian Minister.

Couriers established contact with the Norwegian Government in Norway ; within 24 hours the shipping control machinery was working. British consuls everywhere were instructed to advance money to Norwegian captains when needful. Soon afterwards the Norwegian Government issued a decree requisitioning all Norwegian ships—a decree discussed in the small hours in a London hotel with at least one of the party—a lawyer—sitting in his pyjamas. The Norwegian Government has contracted with the British Ministry of War Transport that all voyages and cargoes should be for the war effort. The Ministry charters the ships from the Government and the agreements regulate the money paid for the ships' use.

Emergency meetings were also held with the representatives of Holland and Belgium, when those countries were invaded, and later with the Greek and Yugoslav representatives. At these meetings quick decisions had to be taken resulting in arrangements to keep hundreds of Allied ships at sea under charter to the British Government. (In fact, the earliest agreement of all was made with some Yugoslav owners in October 1939.) Arrangements regarding French, Polish, Danish, and neutral ships have a similar object. The Allied representatives who took these decisions had to rise to great responsibilities with little time for preparation. Allied Ministers in London, members of their Governments who were available, and leading shipowners such as Mr. Hudig for Holland, and Mr. Lusi for Greece, all helped to reorganise their countries' shipping to continue the fight against the invader.

Of the types of ships serving us, 50 per cent. of the Norwegian ships are tankers; the Greeks are all tramps; the Dutch are predominantly a liner fleet, of the highest importance for military operations, but there are smaller ships, too, rendering vital service around our coast and in the East; on a smaller scale, Belgian vessels are serving similar purposes. Many of the Danish vessels are former fruit carriers. The French have several liners engaged on trooping, and many cargo ships. Their numbers have steadily grown, for, from time to time, a French vessel met at sea has been persuaded to join us. Moreover, a large number of French ships were in North Africa, a few tankers among them, and these are now on charter to us or to America, manned by French crews.

The Poles, who had sent most of their ocean-going ships out of the Baltic in good time, have some ships well suited to trooping; the Yugoslav vessels are cargo ships.

We have built up a good companionship with foreign shipowners and crews. The foreign ships in our service form an integral part of the pool available for the war effort, carrying out the jobs assigned to them exactly as do our own ships. Allied merchant ships have taken part in all the major operations.

8. Wartime Cargoes

A SHIP is an islet compact of men, machinery, cargo and stores. War complicates her existence extremely. The devilries of man are added to the dangers of the sea. Unexampled voyages demand new bunkering ports; the ship may have to lie off a coast instead of in dock; cranes and derricks may not be available or be too small; water may be short, the route may be so devious and lengthy that stores four times normal size must be carried; and the cargo may be just about the last which would have been chosen had choice been free.

There was a ship which took 97 days to get to Trinidad, and she was not square-rigged either. She was a steamer in this war. It was a remarkable Odyssey. Another ship sailed to England from India, and she came round Cape Horn and up the east coast of South America. Soldiers on their way to West Africa or Suez here found themselves venturing towards the Arctic or approaching South America. Men have sailed almost off the map to reach a place that did not look, at first glance, too inaccessible: consider, for example, journeying to Russia via the Persian Gulf. To voyage to Tripoli via the Cape, as we did for a short time, was equivalent to going more than half-way round the world. The 12,000-mile route to Suez to supply our Middle East armies has become historic.

It was not, however, routeing officers who had developed madness, but only the world at large. Routes have been either the safest at the time or the best for other good reasons. They have sometimes sprung from the need to make the best or most economical use of ships. That need has, on occasion, directed ships homeward bound from India to journey to Central America, thence to carry, perhaps, bauxite to North America, and there to reload for home. Or ships have gone in ballast to the Dominions as the quickest means of getting precious cargoes back. Ships' Masters must have found an occasional voyage perplexing, or worse ; and many a ship has sailed in waters she was never built for.

As for the cargoes carried, he was not an ill-tempered man who said they get " nastier and nastier". He was not a stevedore nor yet a crane- or winch-driver, nor yet the docker himself, any of whom may sweat over the tough job of stowing away a 9-ton army vehicle between decks with only six inches to spare. You can see these mighty lorries, swung over (with many a " Whoa ! " and " Steady, Harry ! " and " This way, Jim ! "), poised in mid-air, and then dropped gently down and driven inches this way or that in the hold by the soldier with " M.C." (movement control) on his arm, and marvel at what is done. Any of these men might have used the words ; so might the ship's Master, or the First Officer. But it was none of these. He was merely a shipping man working for the Government, a man whose work is with diagrams and measurements. He was thinking of the problem by and large. He said : " We're combining coal and air-craft now That sounds comic, doesn't it ? " As a shipping man, that tickled him. He said : " In loading vehicles, we try to turn the ship into what's virtually a three-decked garage". One of the first tasks, of course, is to measure up the ships at the ports, see exactly what they will take. Things are being done which the experts said were impossible—carrying tanks between decks, for instance. They said the structure of the ships would not stand it ; but they are standing it. It had to be done.

The shipping expert discussed tanks further. Tanks in the ship are now placed on pedestals, otherwise you could not secure them firmly enough. The tanks' springs played the devil in the beginning ; once or twice there were " rogue tanks " running about the ship, tanks that had broken loose. Bren carriers were crushed like concertinas. All that has

DECKS PACKED WITH AIRCRAFT SHEATHED AGAINST

WEATHER AND CROWDING THE GUNNERS ON THEIR PLATFORM, AN OIL TANKER BRINGS HOME HER CARGO

been overcome. He mentioned experiments. Gradually, what was experimental has become the rule and rules have been modified accordingly—for example, carrying vehicles with petrol already loaded into them. That risk was taken by some ships going to North Africa ; a few fires were started, but they were put out.

More and more cargoes have to be borne on deck because no hatches are big enough to take some of the articles. Ninety-ton locomotives can be found on deck, and Sherman tanks—tanks not under tarpaulins but hermetically sealed against wind and water at the vulnerable spots. But these deck cargoes and the plates to prevent them shifting, combined with the weight of extra armament, create new problems of stability. And stability is a ticklish problem. A ship not ballasted properly may roll precariously in heavy weather. On the other hand, if she is too heavy down below and too stiff, then that will throw the deck cargo about, for she will come out of a roll too fast. It is necessary to compensate deck cargoes with extra weight down below ; but it may also be necessary to counteract a terrible weight and stiffness below with an additional load up above, so that a ship has been known to carry several hundred tons of sand ballast on deck ! Moreover, ballast is not always available at the overseas unloading port ; and in that case, if the vessel is returning without cargo, she is ballasted on the way out so that she can return in proper trim and without delay.

In addition to all this, in summer, and with cargoes deemed not too dangerous, ships are loaded six or 12 inches deeper into the water than in peace time, to carry an extra 500 tons. A ship sails with most stability when she is somewhere near her proper line, when she is " full and down ". Full and down is devoutly to be wished, but often hard to come by. For normal cargoes occupy 50 cubic feet to the ton ; but military cargoes make only a ton with 80 cubic feet, so that steel is often used as ballast even in ships carrying American troops. A ship can be " down "

ON DECK	1	2 Mark IV tanks	1	Four 3-ton
UPPER TWEEN DECK	2	40 tons 250-lb. bombs	2	270 tons fla floats
	3	11 Scout cars	3	Eighteen 3-t
	4	9 trailers	4	4 Daimler armoured
	5	2 AA guns		
LOWER TWEEN DECK	6	Twenty-two 15-cwt. trucks	5	270 tons flar
			6	200 tons W/ stores
			7	120 tons bor tail units
			8	75 tons steel
HOLD	7	6 scout cars	9	15 trailers
	8	50 tons tank spares	10	510 tons mix ammunitio (shells & b
	9	50 tons 25-lb. shells		
	10	160 tons gun stores		

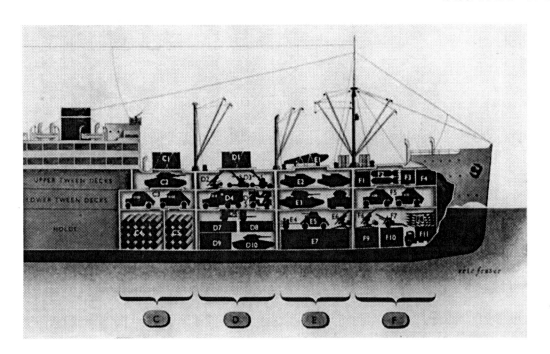

	C		D		E		F	
1	4 cased Spitfires	**1**	2 cased Anson trainers	**1**	2 uncased Boston bombers			ON DECK
2	14 Crusader tanks	**2**	Three 3.7 guns	**2**	24 Bren carriers	**1**	170 tons R.A.F. stores	UPPER TWEEN DECK
		3	24 Bofors			**2**	11 torpedoes	
						3	40 tons wireless gear	
						4	130 tons ordnance stores	
3	Twenty 15-cwt. trucks	**4**	Seven 6-wheeled trucks	**3**	16 Covenanter tanks	**5**	Fifteen 15-cwt. trucks	LOWER TWEEN DECK
		5	22 Jeeps (stowed double tier)					
4	(Deep tank 1) cased petrol	**6**	6 trailers	**4**	9 trailers	**6**	Two 3.7 guns	HOLD
5	(Deep tank 2) cased petrol	**7**	300 tons ammo.	**5**	9 Humber cars	**7**	Twelve 25-lb. guns	
		8	6 cases aircraft wings	**6**	Four 3.7 guns	**8**	200 tons steel pylons	
		9	5 cased Spitfires	**7**	600 tons mixed ammunition	**9**	220 tons tank spares	
		10	20 Crusader tanks			**10**	200 tons 25-lb. ammo.	
						11	One 3-ton store lorry	

WAR CARGO. This diagram shows in detail the typical cargo of an outgoing liner of 10,500 tons. Loading must take into account balance, safety, accessibility, and speed of discharge. Around the items indicated above another 5,000 tons of general stores are stowed wherever space allows. Loading officers ring many changes in the general arrangement shown here.

TANKS FOR THE DESERT   LOCOMOTIVES FOR TRANSPORT

with half her space empty, and too light with all her space full : lead stores at 12 to 15 cubic feet a ton, but sisal at 70 cubic feet. A ship whose main cargo is wool may float after being torpedoed, when she is one-half empty ; but a ship down to her marks with ore will sink like a stone, for sea will swiftly fill the empty spaces. " Oh for ' sea-kindly ' cargoes ! " may murmur the shipowner and Master ; but they grin and bear it, getting as near towards performing the miracle as they can. In this spirit a new tanker has once or twice carried a cargo of wheat, or when loaded with oil has taken an extra 500 tons of general cargo in a forward hold. In the last two years tankers have been seen with an extra top deck on which were placed landing craft, aircraft, tanks and other cargoes. Banana boats have at times in this war brought frozen meat and bacon to this country.

Lifts are a dominant problem. Ships' derricks have to be constantly stiffened, for the tendency is for derricks to weaken by wear as lifts get bigger. And lifts do get bigger. Railway engines weigh up to 120 tons. The old-time derrick of a tramp ship lifted five tons, the exceptional one 15 tons. But all new ships are fitted with a derrick that will lift 50 tons, and some ships not new have been fitted with them also. The percentage of cargo which is technically known as " heavy lift " has increased considerably in the course of the past two years—from 7 per cent. to 45 per cent. To deal with this, crane ships have been built—ships which can themselves lift weights from 80 to 120 tons, ships with special tanks to counter-act a vessel's tendency to list when she undertakes this heavy work. Movable cranes have been built on barges, and sometimes two or more barges rigged together to mount derricks lifting up to 50 tons. Cranes have been transported from the east coast of Britain to the west ; a 150-ton crane has been towed from the south coast to Scotland.

All this—the control, new routeing and strange loading of ships—is a part of the war-time metamorphosis of merchant ships into Merchant Navy. The shipowner himself takes his important part and (maybe with a wry smile to himself) reflects on how he

OIL FOR THE AIR FORCE

is helping to reverse the shipowner's dream, as it were. He has tried his hardest, for example, to convince some of our Dominions that they should be content to get what they want from the United States rather than from us. Gone is the old-time ideal of striving to meet all the demands made ; for the demands themselves are no longer free. Trade no longer finds its own channels. Peoples have had to be taught to build on a programme, to plan ahead, and to realise that failing to do so would result in wants not being supplied. In the beginning we had a policy of maintaining certain exports ; and after sending men and supplies to France, Egypt, India and Singapore we had a partial return to normal carrying. But not for long. Moreover, such elements as the policy of Lend-Lease, the decreasing importance of currency, the manpower question—all exercised their influence at various times. Concurrent with them, restrictions grew more firm ; within twelve months of the outbreak of war, freedom of trade was strangled and the shipping men had played their part in tightening the knot.

Some description has been given in earlier pages of what must be done before a convoy can sail. Similarly, every convoy reaching Britain demands immense preparation—for unloading, for transhipment of cargo by coasters, or its transport by road or rail or inland water.

Every ship when she arrives in port is scheduled for a named outward convoy. A major problem is the co-ordination of various programmes of unloading, repairing, arming, bunkering and reloading, all of it complicated by the need for seeing that officers and men get proper rest and leave after the strain of the voyage. If a ship misses her scheduled convoy, the fact is recorded and studied, in order that, if possible, it may not happen again. In every principal convoy-assembly port, the same check is maintained.

A primary decision taken before arrival is that which allots ships to the various ports, a decision which is taken a week or so before the vessels are due, but may—because of air bombardment, or for other reasons—be varied or modified later.

The " Shipping Diversion Room ", where

TRUCKS FOR BATTLE   BOMBERS FOR THE RUHR

these decisions are taken, has functioned since September 1st, 1939. The room has never been left unoccupied, either by day or night, from that date onwards.

It is in the morning that the principal meeting occurs, a meeting of some 40 men representing the Ministries of Food and Supply, the British Army, Navy and Air Force, the United States Forces, our National Dock Labour organisation, our coastal shipping, our railways, roads and canals, and the various United Kingdom ports. The chairman is a well-known business man, in peace time director of a British line of steamships. He acts almost as a judge. He sits at the centre of a long, rectangular table, with his clerk alongside. The room is workmanlike, a bit dingy ; there are several maps on the walls ; the appointments are few.

On this particular morning the problem is a convoy of 73 ships, reduced, however, by a few which have returned to their port of origin. It is the task of these men to feed our home ports with ships to their full capacity ; in general, no ship is sent to the east coast if it can be dealt with in the west. A phrase

is used : " This little pocket handkerchief of a country".

First, the chairman reads out a weather forecast, and next he tells of casualties to ships. Such-and-such is sunk ; another damaged may be still afloat—she has got water in the hold ; a third has been torpedoed on the starboard side—three survivors have been picked up. He reports an air raid on a certain coast.

We turn now to the list before us. It gives the name of each ship, her tonnage, speed, draught fore and aft, and the cargo she is bringing. Sometimes the cargo is entirely aviation spirit, but in other ships it is infinitely varied. One ship is carrying wheat, lumber, aluminium, cheese, motor trucks, steel alloy, chemicals, electrodes, guns, flax and tank parts ; a second brings shells, bombs, T.N.T., dried fruits and landing craft ; and a third, steel, sugar, powder, T.N.T., starch, copper, lumber, cotton, landing craft and orange juice.

The secretary reads out the name of the ship. A port for it has been suggested on the list before us ; but the representative of

FOOD FOR THE HOME FRONT

that port may say that he cannot handle a certain part of the cargo—possibly explosives. Other ports are thereupon discussed and the right one found. As the work goes on, phrases spring from this or that man :

" This steel."—" Yes, we'll take 2,000 of that."

" Locomotives."—" Yes, we can handle those."

" There are 78 heavy lifts the ship won't be able to deal with. . . ."

" Extensive repairs needed. Discharge her at anchorage."

" How many explosives ships have you now ? "—" Four."

" You'll have to scream for it."—" We *have* screamed for it."

" She's Clyde for orders."

" Two hundred tons for the South—they'll go by coaster."

" A lot of that copper is for South Wales."

" You'll have to wait a day for tides."— " No, can't do that, she'll have to go elsewhere."

Occasionally the secretary says, " That'll be by order "—meaning by order of this committee. Such an order changes the instruction in the ship Master's possession.

The problems themselves have grown, as imports have grown ; a tough one arises when a ship carries bulk cargo, half of which is bound for the east coast and half for the west. In the period when our ports were being bombed with some regularity, the room occasionally went into session at short notice, diverting cargoes hither and thither.

Immense care is taken to conceal ship movements. Messages from this room to the ports are sent in code ; ships are not mentioned—instructions are given merely to be ready to handle such and such cargo.

As to the length of time ships are in our ports, this is a complex business dependent on convoy intervals, among other factors. Heavy lifts—tanks, landing craft and so on— are increasing in number, masking a part of the improved working at the ports. Weather can make or mar an unloading. The aim is to save ships' time in turn-round and to make the most economical use of labour and plant. Time spent in port, however, in general, has diminished steadily.

9. Ships in the Thick of it

EVERY British merchant ship has been busily engaged in the war from the day it began—her owners and the British Government have seen to that—but there are some that by nature of circumstance, or by good fortune in avoiding damage, have been in the thick of it more than others.

The purpose here is to record without elaboration the war activities of two or three vessels which can stand as examples of what many other ships have achieved. The *City of Hereford*, for instance, voyaged on the eve of war to Gibraltar and South Africa. After returning to this country she sailed to the United States. From Montreal she made several voyages to Calcutta, proceeding next to Suez where she narrowly escaped being blown up in the canal—the preceding ship hit a mine and lost her stern in the explosion. She now sailed to India and returned thence to Britain to take part in a Malta convoy. In February 1942 she was in the East Indies. After that she attempted to reach Malta from Suez and, on the convoy being withdrawn, sailed to America to bring home cargo " topped off " (in her Master's phrase) " by bombers and explosives ". The ship endured many attacks in various seas by German, Italian and Japanese aircraft, and U-boats one of which in the Atlantic she nearly rammed. In Batavia the Master notes : " We took H.M.S. *Rover* (a damaged submarine from Singapore) in tow, and went off to sea in a large convoy for Indian ports ". One of her Malta convoys was very lively. A pack of some 20 E-boats delivered at night a rush attack from both sides. Many were sunk by our combined salvos, and our ships sailed into port to the music of the flagship's band playing "A life on the ocean wave ".

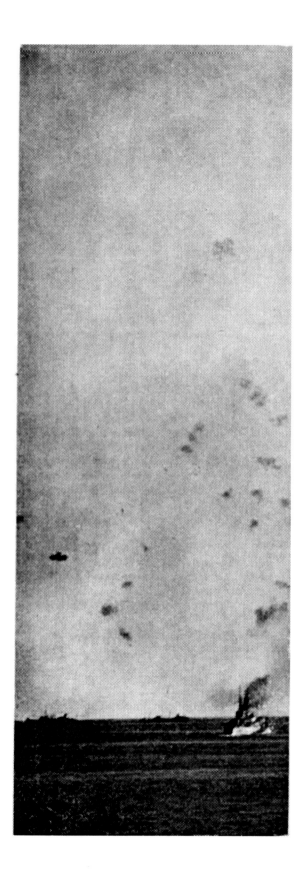

The liner *Destro* (Captain Stanley Johnson, O.B.E.) was first attacked in the Ægean Sea in June 1940 ; she continued to work in the Eastern Mediterranean till March 1942. During that time she was attacked by enemy bombers or dive-bombers no fewer than a hundred times, and it may be far more. She suffered near misses on 20 or 30 occasions. Her guns hit an enemy bomber in Salamis Straits outside Piræus harbour, and probably accounted for two more in Tobruk harbour in 1942. In Suda Bay she was continuously bombed for a fortnight ; in Tobruk she endured during one stay 68 bombing raids. At least six times she suffered damage ; once, fires were started on board ; and in Tobruk harbour three of the crew were killed and six wounded. She was attacked by a submarine in convoy and fired at the U-boat ; and she was shelled, by mistake, by our own shore batteries in Crete.

The m.v. *Coxwold* (Captain R. Pratt, M.B.E.), a small ship of 1,600 tons, is a coaster, never meant for the deep-sea trade, but she has been adventuring afar and doing dangerous work carrying cased petrol for the Forces since a fortnight after war broke out. She was at Narvik when the situation was at its gravest and she was busy in the North Africa expedition as far east as Bougie and Bone. She was at one time so far forward along the coast that neither the Army nor R.A.F. had arrived, and the port was in charge of a naval officer whose ship had been sunk. Between Narvik and North Africa, she ran to Iceland at one time and Gibraltar at another.

The *Coxwold* has been in the North Atlantic in the depths of winter, had ships sunk round her and gone to their help, taking off on one occasion the Commodore and his staff. The latter, after being aboard her 15 days, wrote : " I thought she was a wonderful little ship and her behaviour in very bad weather remarkable. I have never known a captain who stuck to the bridge as hers did. I gave up trying to get him to go down and rest".

The tramp ship *Dan-y-Bryn* (Captain Hugh MacLeod, D.S.C.,) had war adventures before her voyages to Murmansk and Archangel. She shot part of the wing from a Heinkel in the North Sea early in 1940, fought a six-hour battle with a submarine in the Caribbean the same year, and scored hits on a surface raider on the way home from Vancouver. During her voyages to Russia she shot down 18 enemy aircraft.

Another tramp ship, the *Briarwood* (Captain W. H. Lawrence, C.B.E.), sailed in one or two of the same convoys to Russia as the *Dan-y-Bryn* and equally distinguished herself in fights with the enemy elsewhere, shooting down two aircraft in the English Channel as early as May 1940, and a third while sailing alone from Gibraltar to New York in August 1941. In convoys to Russia she shot down two more Ju. 88s.

The *Briarwood's* war service began with transporting men and stores of the first British Expeditionary Force to St. Nazaire, but in November 1939 she was transferred to the Narvik trade to carry iron ore. She was one of the last ships to leave that port before the enemy arrived. She was now degaussed and put on the North Atlantic trade, where she sailed in the famous *Jervis Bay* convoy. She made four further voyages in the North Atlantic trade, and saw ships torpedoed. Thereafter she sailed with coal for Portugal and was again attacked both by bomber and U-boat, but not damaged. She now sailed to New York alone, returned to Britain and was fitted for the North Russian convoy—this in October 1941. On leaving Iceland for Russia during a strong gale and in darkness she damaged her bow on an iceberg ; an Admiralty diver plugged the outside and the crew filled the bows with cement and two weeks later she set off once more. In Russia two ice-breakers were needed to get her into port. Two days later two ice-breaking tugs broke the *Briarwood* out of harbour again, but it took 16 days to move 70 miles. No cargo or ballast being available, she drew but 3 feet 6 inches

STRUCK TO THE HEART. She has been found alone in the South Atlantic by a surface raider. There is only one end for her. A torpedo, fired from close range, breaks her in two.

forward and 14 feet 6 inches aft, and in order to keep the propeller below the ice her after-hold was flooded with water, which promptly froze in. She had to be dry-docked and repaired before her next Arctic voyage could begin.

In March 1942 she sailed for Russia again, her Master acting this time as Vice-Commodore ; in heavy attacks from the air she shot down an aircraft both on the voyage out and when in Murmansk, the second aircraft crashing on the docks alongside. This convoy completed, the *Briarwood* returned to the North Atlantic to bring from America a cargo of ore. On her return Captain Lawrence was given special Admiralty duties, and Captain J. Shaw took her in convoy on her next voyage to Murmansk, which she reached on Christmas Day, 1942,

without incident. The port was raided and U-boat attacks were met on the homeward voyage but the *Briarwood's* good luck held.

Two actions against enemy raiders in Eastern waters may be mentioned here. At dusk on August 20th, 1940, the *Turakina* (Captain J. B. Laird) was attacked by a surface raider in the Tasman Sea. The *Turakina* had only one gun against a well-armed and faster ship, but she fought for two and a half hours before going down with colours flying. Before leaving Sydney, Captain J. B. Laird had said that, if attacked, he would fight to the end. He was killed during the action.

The second action was fought by the m.v. *Ondina* (Captain William Horsman), a tanker of 14,000 tons, in support of H.M.I.S. *Bengal* against two Japanese raiders on November

73

NOT A CHANCE. In a wide sea empty of help, a British merchant ship goes down before the guns of the battleship *Graf Spee.* Casually the German crew stand watching.

11th, 1942. A few minutes after first sighting the enemy, the *Bengal* ordered the *Ondina* to turn away and proceed independently, giving her a rendezvous for 24 hours later. The *Bengal* turned to port to intercept and challenge. She received a broadside in reply from Raider No. 1, which was rapidly closing range, while Raider No. 2 remained in the background. *Bengal* opened fire but her shots fell short. Five minutes later, the *Ondina* now at 8,000 yards distance, and determined to do what she could, entered the fight with her 4-inch gun, but her shells fell over the target. She thereupon dropped her range by 400 yards and her fifth shot scored a hit, causing a violent explosion, which threw into the air the debris of two aircraft housed on the raider's after-deck and, in addition, causing fire to break out. Raider No. 1,

thus stung, divided her fire henceforward between the *Bengal* and the *Ondina*, and soon shot away the *Ondina's* topmast and main aerial. The *Bengal* was, of course, still firing. *Ondina's* shooting became increasingly good. She claimed five hits in swift succession on the bridge, midship superstructure and the stern, and now a violent explosion occurred in the Japanese ship, blowing off the stern completely, and she began to sink ; her bows lifted in the air and the ship became almost vertical.

Raider No. 2 now became prominent in the fight, and eventually shifted her fire from the *Bengal* to the *Ondina*. The *Ondina's* ammunition was running short and she used her remaining 12 shots without effect. Being now without ammunition and unable to fight, Captain Horsman hoisted two white

FIRE ON THE WATER. Another ship, upending, and with only her bows in sight is sucked down through the blazing pool of her own oil into the depths below

sheets. This did not stop the Japanese from continuing to fire and almost at once shrapnel burst on the bridge and killed Captain Horsman, who had just given the order to abandon ship. Raider No. 2 approached nearer still, firing, and when about 400 yards distant she launched two torpedoes, which struck the *Ondina's* after-tanks. She took a list of 30 degrees to starboard and must have seemed doomed. The Japanese now machine-gunned men in the boats and rafts, killing the chief engineer and two Chinese, and before departing fired a further torpedo and two shells into the *Ondina*.

But the *Ondina* still floated and the second Officer, Mr. Bartele Bakker, who had controlled the 4-inch gun in the fight, accompanied by the third engineer, two A.B.s and three Chinese, returned to the ship

to see what could be done to save her. A fire was quenched, the port tanks were flooded to put her in trim, steam was raised, the remainder of the crew taken back on board and six days later she reached Fremantle, 1,400 miles away. Among those who had distinguished themselves was Ah Kong, the Chinese quartermaster, who had been at the wheel during the action. He was awarded the D.S.M.

A large number of actions against submarines have been fought by merchant ships several of which have achieved success. As day broke on April 21st, 1941, Mr. A. Lidguard, chief officer of the tramp ship *Empire Storm*, sighted a suspicious craft on the port bow steering across from port to starboard. Captain G. W. Stephenson, O.B.E., D.S.C., going to the bridge, made her out to be a

"ONE SHIP OF THE CONVOY WAS LOST". Torpedoed at night in the North Atlantic, a Norwegian ship, laden with ammunition, blows up. Top left, fire spurts out the moment the torpedo strikes her. Four minutes later it was growing with the steady persistence of sunrise. In another eight minutes, ship and cargo were destroyed in one shattering explosion.

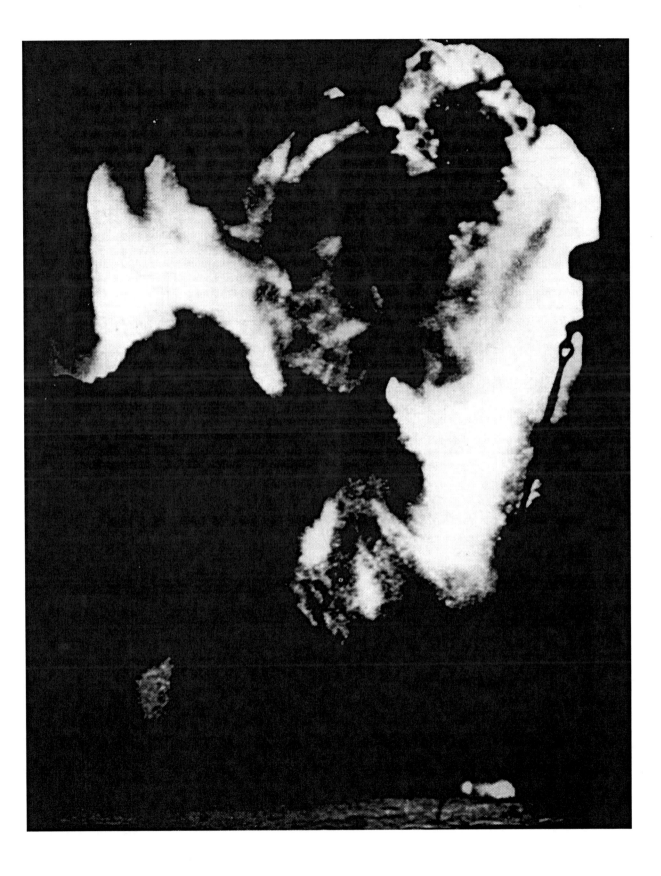

U-boat 500 feet off and travelling at a good speed. The alarm signal was rung and he tried to ram the U-boat, but she was too fast. Fire was then opened with tracer from the bridge machine-gun and the bullets were seen to bounce off her deck. This gave direction for the 4-inch gun, which was now laid on her. With the first shell the U-boat was struck at the base of the conning tower. The range was no more than 600 yards. She at once dived, but within a few minutes surfaced and appeared to be stopped. More shells were fired and she was hit again, this time at the after-end of the conning tower. The U-boat began to sink by the stern, and 40 minutes after she was first seen her bows rose out of the water and she rolled and vanished at an angle of 50 degrees. Six rounds of 4-inch had been fired and one of 12-pounder. The U-boat did not fire a shot. Two escort ships now reached the scene and dropped depth charges.

Another successful action was fought, beginning at 12.35 p.m. on October 19th, 1939, by the tramp ship *Rockpool* (Captain W. H. Harland, O.B.E.). A U-boat opened fire on the ship's starboard beam, and the helm was at once put over hard a-port. All hands went to action stations and a radio message was dispatched. The submarine fired four or five rounds in quick succession but did not score a hit. The *Rockpool* now brought her gun to bear and opened fire. After her third shot the U-boat submerged. She was not down long. After only a few minutes she surfaced again, and as soon as her periscope was showing the *Rockpool* began to shell her again. A duel of fire now began, shrapnel from the submarine bursting just clear of the merchant ship's bows, and spray from the *Rockpool's* rounds bursting over the U-boat's conning tower. Once or twice she submerged, only to surface and continue shooting. The battle went on for an hour and ten minutes before the *Rockpool* eluded her. But that was not the end. The *Rockpool* had so damaged the U-boat that she could not submerge for long, and a destroyer, which came in answer to the merchantman's signal, sank the U-boat and captured the survivors.

Not all our merchantmen carried a gun in the autumn of 1939. The *Clan MacBean* (Captain E. Coultas, O.B.E.), a cargo-liner,

STORM CAN DESTROY AS SAVAGELY AS A TORPEDO. ROCK CAN REND AS SURELY AS A MINE

had no defence except seamanship when she was attacked. She was sailing independently, since her convoy had been scattered the day before. The U-boat fired a torpedo from three-quarters of a mile away, two points on the port bow. The merchantman's chief officer put the helm hard over and the torpedo narrowly missed the bow. The U-boat now surfaced and tried to reach a position on the merchantman's quarter, but the *Clan MacBean* evaded this and kept her ahead, bringing the U-boat within danger of being rammed. The merchantman steamed to within 200 feet and, although the submarine opened fire with three rounds of shell, every shot missed : suddenly, sensing she was in danger of being rammed, she dived ; her gun crew were left in the water crying out loudly. The merchant ship passed right over the U-boat but she was already too deep to be rammed and was later seen astern picking up such of her men as she could.

In the following month the tramp ship *Hopestar* (Captain J. Steward, O.B.E.) engaged a submarine for six hours about 150 miles off Land's End. The fight began shortly before noon, in a heavy sea with a strong westerly wind. The first torpedo from the starboard quarter missed by five yards owing to helm being put hard a-port. The *Hopestar* now steered an irregular, zigzag course, and opened fire on the U-boat every time she was sighted. All possible speed was made, but two hours after the first torpedo was sighted a second was observed coming on the port bow, bucking on top of the waves ; it missed the ship's stern by only two yards. As a ruse the ship now hoisted a signal by flags saying to an imaginary warship : " Submarine attacking from the stern". An hour and a half after the second torpedo, a third was seen running from the port quarter; again it passed extremely near, a matter of two yards. The *Hopestar's* shells now burst very close to the submarine's conning tower, and she hurriedly submerged. This was the last seen of her ; dusk coming on, and a

smoke screen made by dropped floats, enabled the merchantman to elude further attack.

Our little ships, or curious ships, have adventured so far across the sea to such unaccustomed places that those who met them might well have thought them lost or manned by men bereft of their senses.

A voyage of particular valiance was that of the *Al Garna*, a self-propelled steam-crane lighter which sailed from Port Glasgow to the Middle East, occupying 328 days on the way—rather longer than it took Vasco da Gama to sail in 1497 from Portugal round the Cape and discover India. But da Gama had no such particular problems as beset the *Al Garna*. It is unlikely, for example, that his vessel sailed with both fore and aft ends under water, as happened to the *Al Garna* whenever there was any size of sea, or that the discomfort below decks in bad weather was quite so great, for on the crane ship all vents had then to be closed to prevent flooding. Her preparation for the 12,000-mile journey needed much work. She was unwieldy and small and her freeboard very low. The sheerlegs had to be dismantled and additional space found for bunkers, stores and water. The midship section was made watertight, and a V-shaped breakwater 2 feet 6 inches high built forward. Heavy weather met with on the first stage of the voyage damaged both superstructure and breakwater and she had to go into dry dock before proceeding. When the voyage was half over, her Master wrote that the only incentive to carry on was pride of profession and knowing he had never yet failed in anything. Once more part of the superstructure was damaged by seas and the lagging on steam piping to winches washed away. Over the final stage, owing to bad coal, she had to be assisted by tow. But she reached her port, her crew nearly a year older than when they left Scotland.

Ferries and port tugs have made voyages as long in mileage if not in time, usually crossing 2,000 miles of open Atlantic before reaching the West Coast on their way to more distant ports. Every one of them has reached her journey's end.

One of them was the *Empire Warlock*, a tug of 253 tons, sailed from the Clyde to Suez by Captain R. Geyton. The task was as new to him as the voyage was to the tug, for he is a Master of tankers, but they both did what was required. The *Empire Warlock* worked her passage, so to speak, for she took in tow from South Wales two French submarine chasers, towing them on separate lines. It was a co-operative effort, for during parts of the journey—when nearing Gibraltar or approaching Bathurst—the Frenchmen cast off and acted as escorts to the tug. In the Gambia river, the tug pulled off the *Zouave* (Captain W. H. Cambridge), which had gone ashore, and at Freetown in company with another tug she took a crane barge with a crane 85 feet high to Takoradi, a distance of 933 miles. She arrived at Walvis Bay pulling a lighter. The naval officer in charge remarked that Captain Geyton looked a very superior person to be in command of a tug, to which Captain Geyton replied : " Maybe, but this is a very superior tug". Five and a half months after starting he reached Suez.

These are a handful of the 10,000 small craft which the Sea Transport Department of the Ministry of War Transport has requisitioned or bought during the war for a variety of purposes, from the victualling of naval ships to the provision of water-borne sites for balloons. Others serve as minesweepers, fire floats and in many other capacities. When the threat of invasion was gravest, hundreds of small craft were moored at intervals on the Norfolk Broads and on our large reservoirs, and yet others patrolled Lake Windermere and like stretches of inland water.

In these small craft scattered over the world 85 per cent. of the crews are still civilians. Their achievements in towing take their place in history. Slowly, through dangerous water assailed by wind and sea, they have tugged and persuaded the blunt and intractable halves of torpedoed ships.

Our hospital ships, of which we have had 55 in this war, are navigated, engineered and manned by the Merchant Navy. It is the merchant seamen's task to take these ships of mercy, with their sick and wounded, their doctors, nurses and other medical staffs and equipment, on their lawful occasions to and from the various battlefronts. They were at Dunkirk, Tobruk, Malta, Rangoon, Algiers, and every other storm centre ; and in most

of them they were shelled, bombed or machine-gunned.

Of the 55 ships, 39 belonged before the war to the British Mercantile Marine, among them passenger liners, cargo-passenger ships and vessels on railway service to the Channel Isles, Ireland and the Continent. Many ships' captains, officers and men who sailed them in peace, have continued to serve them during the war. The Royal Navy has its hospital ships attached to the fleets; military hospital carriers more usually transport wounded from a battlefront to a base. Quite often wounded have been taken from theatres of war to hospitals in South Africa or Australia or New Zealand; but from North Africa they have, of course, often been brought home. Not only does the Merchant Navy man the hospital ships, but ships' owners or managers are responsible

THIS WAS A SHIP. Lying in a British port, she was loading explosives for the Middle East. With 350 tons of bombs on board she was hit in a night raid, burned for nine hours and then blew up.

for feeding the patients in accordance with diets laid down, and for providing messing of medical staffs.

Nine hospital ships have been sunk by the enemy—the *Brighton* and *Maid of Kent* in Dieppe Harbour in May 1940, the *Paris* when sailing to Dunkirk in June 1940, the *Ramb IV* when taking 269 sick and wounded from Tobruk to Alexandria in May 1942, the *Centaur* off Australia in May 1943, the *Talamba* off Sicily in July 1943, the *Newfoundland* and the *St. David* off Naples in September 1943 and January 1944 respectively, and the *Amsterdam* off Normandy in August 1944. About 13 others have been damaged in enemy attacks; the *Llandovery Castle* has been damaged twice in five bombing attacks ; the *Somersetshire* has been torpedoed in addition to being bombed three times ; the *Isle of Guernsey* has been shelled by shore batteries, dive-bombed and torpedo-bombed ; the *St. Julien*, and the *St. Andrew* have all been shelled and bombed more than once. Others which have been hit are the *Leinster, Worthing, Dorsetshire, Dinard, Isle of Thanet, Aba, Vita* and the *Karapara*. All these vessels were, of course, flying the Red Cross flag and bearing the customary markings of hospital ships in accordance with the Geneva Convention. A hospital ship bombed and damaged in Tobruk was twice attacked when in tow shortly afterwards.

A note may be added, on the actual events when the *Ramb IV* was set on fire in the Mediterranean on May 10th, 1942. It comes from the chief engineer. " It was her ninth or tenth trip to Tobruk ", he said. " We had already brought away about 3,000 casualties. On one occasion we loaded 300 wounded in 1 hour 55 minutes, which was, I think, a record. We did it by barges and by direct loading also. May 10th was a Sunday and we were all at breakfast when the air attack was made. The ship had her big awnings up bearing the Red Cross, in addition to the usual markings. One bomb struck B ward and caused a great fire. By the time it was extinguished nothing was left but white

ashes ; even the iron bedsteads had been consumed. Just one tin hat lay there. We kept the ship's head to the wind to prevent the flames spreading. We didn't abandon the ship till midday—not till five of the six tanks had exploded. We estimated that about 180 of the wounded were burned to death."

Members of the Merchant Navy crews have been killed or wounded in these enemy attacks. An able seaman was wounded by machine-gun fire when climbing down a rope ladder to rescue an airman who had baled out.

The *Atlantis* may stand as one example of what a busy hospital ship has done. She has steamed 230,000 miles and carried over 20,000 wounded and sick. Early in 1940 she brought invalids from Alexandria to the United Kingdom ; her next voyages were between Britain and Norway, where she was bombed at anchor both off Skaanland and in Skellesvick Bay. In September 1940 she was again in the Middle East, and in 1941 was operating between the Middle East, South Africa and Bombay. The next year saw her making voyages between Suez, South Africa and Aden, returning to Britain in November 1942 with over 600 sick and wounded. Since then she has twice sailed to New York with American and Canadian invalids and thence to Durban, returning once more to Britain.

Other ships have done fine work but travelled less. The hospital carrier *Isle of Jersey*, for instance, a small ship of some 2,000 tons, has been in attendance on the Home Fleet, anchored most of her time but making occasional voyages to Aberdeen. Of high adventure she has seen little, of bad weather much, of monotony more than her share.

But when the Normandy landings occurred she sailed into the main stream of war. She was one of ten such hospital carriers used in the opening phase. Later there were twelve. The removal of wounded from the beaches was a task for which they were supremely

LAME DUCK. Smoking and crippled, she labours into the harbour mouth. Her steering is gone, she is down by the stern. The rescue tug will take her in tow and nurse her to the quayside.

suited. Not only did the Merchant Navy man them, but they manned also the water ambulances—a quartermaster and two A.B.s to each—which plied between shore and ship across two to seven miles of sea, a strip of water often under fire and at one period swept by a gale. Most of the hospital carriers had six of those ambulances and each ambulance took, as a rule, six wounded on stretchers and a handful of others sitting. Very many journeys had to be made.

Among the hospital carriers off Normandy were the *St. Julien* and the *Dinard* both of which were mined but not severely enough to be out of service for more than a few weeks. At a later stage the bigger hospital ships joined in the work.

10. Crash Landings

IT was in November 1940 that the name of the *San Demetrio* was written firmly into the history of the Merchant Navy. Shelled and set ablaze by the German battleship *Deutschland* while sailing in the *Jervis Bay* convoy, the tanker was abandoned. But later on a handful of her crew under the command of Mr. A. G. N. Hawkins, second officer, and Mr. C. Pollard, chief engineer, adrift in a ship's boat, came across the burning vessel, reboarded her, got the engines going, and steering in the fashion known to seamen as " by guess and by God ", brought her to the Clyde. She is the best known of the lame

SHELLED, BURNT, AND MISSHAPEN, abandoned but later reboarded by her crew, the tanker *San Demetrio* came safely to the Clyde.

HALF CAME HOME. The gashe lies beached on the Scottish

ducks which our seamen have brought home when the enemy thought them finished for good ; but she is one of a gallant company. The tradition that a ship is never finished while an outside chance of saving her remains has been staunchly upheld by British seamen in this war, before the *San Demetrio* and since. The high-spirited remark that " so long as she keeps most of the ocean on the outside she'll be all right " has been voiced more than once in times of adversity.

A tale which is comparable with that of the *San Demetrio* can be written of the motor tanker *Franche Comte* (Captain L. C. Church, O.B.E.), which was shelled on the night of March 14th, 1941, and holed in No. 1 port tank, four feet above the water-line. This damage was not serious. Two nights later however, the convoy was again attacked and she was torpedoed, receiving heavy damage to three tanks and the pump-room. She took fire and settled badly by the head. The vessel had to be abandoned ; but Captain Church, who had returned to sea after an absence of six years (and had with him as chief

engineer, M. F. le Roux, a Frenchman, who came to Britain when his country collapsed), was determined to reboard the ship if she did not founder. He and his crew were taken aboard a destroyer ; but some time later Captain Church, accompanied by several officers, engineers, radio officers and the chief steward, tried to pull back to the ship by lifeboat. Wind and sea prevented this and they were taken aboard a corvette. The captain's determination, however, remained, and further volunteers joined him—men who had recently lost their own ships—among them an officer, engineer, gunner and a Norwegian A.B. Once more they set off by boat to the *Franche Comte*, but when they got alongside—it was dark at the time—the fire still burned, and the sight through the hole in her port side was most forbidding. They remained alongside till daybreak. While they were standing off, an armed trawler arrived and picked them up (we may note how well the Royal Navy took care of them), but Captain Church reiterated his wish to remain close by and the trawler's com-

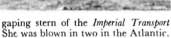

gaping stern of the *Imperial Transport*
She was blown in two in the Atlantic.

WITH AN OPEN TORPEDO-WOUND in her side, and her fo'c'sle awash,
the *Franche Comte* made port with 11,000 tons of oil in her tanks

mander agreed. They reboarded at 9 a.m., by which time the seas had put out the flames, and after two and a half hours' hard work the ship was got under way with her own engines. It was stiff going. Compasses were out of adjustment, she was drawing 33 feet forward and, indeed, so far down by the head that the fo'c'sle was awash. Engines were so tilted that it was extremely difficult to make oil circulate. But the *Franche Comte* forged slowly on, and, in fact, two days later was able to act as good Samaritan by supplying stores to the corvette which had assisted them and had 79 survivors on board. The *Franche Comte* gained port without assistance, bringing in her tanks over 11,000 tons of Admiralty oil.

A third vessel worthy to take her place in this company is the m.v. *Imperial Transport* (Captain W. Smail). Her experience may be unique. When a torpedo struck her in the North Atlantic on February 11th, 1940, and blew her into two pieces, severing her just abaft the bridge, the men on the forepart had barely time to reach the after-end and

some of them jumped two feet over the widening gap of sea. The fore-part drifted away and was lost sight of, but two days later, at 4 o'clock in the afternoon, the rear half (or, rather, two-thirds), which was under way and sailing at about $3\frac{1}{2}$ knots, came upon the fore-end which was still projecting about 50 feet above water. Prompt steps had to be taken to avoid a collision.

Charts and instruments were in the fore-part of the vessel and therefore lost, and for navigation her captain had only an atlas and ruler ; but progress was made. Four destroyers were sighted on the next day and Captain Smail was asked if he wished to abandon ship. The answer was " No", and an escort was thereupon provided and a course set for the north of Scotland. The weather worsened and the ship's steering became faulty, so that she moved in circles. Water was now breaking into the engine-room. But she was not left to her fate ; tugs eventually brought her into the Clyde and a new forepart was built on to her.

It was an ordeal of another sort, but not

85

less trying, that confronted the Master of a well-known liner. When it was over he phrased it thus : " At 1224 G.M.T. we let go the port anchor in Horta Bay—and what a relief ! Seven hundred miles with no stern, rudder or gun, in the North Atlantic in January, an area infested with submarines and within range of the Focke-Wulf Condors ; the ship absolutely alone, 1,400 personnel and crew ; sou'west gales and a high sea running".

A terrific explosion had occurred at 8.15 p.m. when the ship was beginning the second leg of a zigzag course. The torpedo, in the Master's view, hit the shoulder of the rudder, causing it to jump its pintles. The torpedo then moved upwards, killing 24 men and wounding four. The aft gun was blown 12 feet into the air and lost overboard. The Master began to steer the ship by her engines, a method which called for 130 engine-telegraph signals each watch. Sometimes the ship steered to within two points but at others she would " take a sheer off about eight or nine points and sometimes go completely round". There were technical reasons why one engine could not be given " a touch astern " to stop this circular movement. Next morning a Focke-Wulf was seen approaching on the starboard bow, low down. The liner opened fire. Two bombs were dropped which missed by 20 to 30 yards, but a burst from the rear gun injured the boatswain. Hits were scored by the ship and the aircraft was last seen diving into a squall and pouring out black smoke from the tail.

The ship was not in harbour long. Early in February she turned her bow seawards again, having still no rudder or stern, but this time escorted. The voyage had just begun when a destroyer raced through the Fayal Channel at full speed, signalling that she had just rammed and sunk a U-boat and taken 41 prisoners, and asking the liner to do the best speed she could and go northwards, as other U-boats were lurking in wait. " But", says her captain, " ' Elsie,' as she

was known to the escort, refused to play and became very awkward, though she would behave fairly well on about an east-south-east course, which was just what the escort did not want. At dusk that evening the battle royal began, destroyers dropping depth charges, firing guns, throwing up snowflakes and star shells, and the U-boats fighting back. The escort ordered the course to be altered, but again ' Elsie ' refused to play and I was forced to take the Admiralty tug." Altogether she sailed 3,400 miles without stern or rudder. This piece of seamanship is rivalled by that which brought the *Surrey* (Captain F. Lougheed) across a vast stretch of the Atlantic without rudder ; 2,217 miles were covered by adjusting engine revolutions to take advantage of varying winds.

Many a ship has sailed astonishing distances after being torpedoed. The *San Cirilo* (Captain J. Thomson, O.B.E.) was navigated over 14,246 miles before reaching New York, where complete repairs were done. She was attacked south of Colombo, succeeded in reaching Bombay where temporary repairs were carried out, and sailed thence to South Africa and Trinidad. This period occupied six months. She is distinguished also for having had her galley fires extinguished by quantities of petrol ! This petrol was shot into the air in columns when the torpedo struck her, soaking deck planking and boat equipment, filling the deck awnings, and dropping through ventilators and skylights into the engine-room and on to the boiler platform. The petrol fell on the cylinder tops and, as her Master remarks, " It is little short of a miracle that there was neither explosion nor fire". The whole deck bulged four feet upwards for a length of 70 feet from the midship line to the starboard side.

The *San Felix* (Captain G. W. Highley) made another remarkable voyage, for although the distance sailed was less—720 miles—the damage to her was greater ; she had a hole 76 feet long blown in the hull. That was in May 1941. She made port

THE SHIP THAT LIVED AGAIN.   In 1941 the 28,000-ton liner *Georgic* was bombed and burnt out in
Suez harbour.   She was taken to India where, after nine months, she was repaired and refloated.
It was one of the biggest salvage jobs of the war.   Above, the *Georgic* in flames the night after the attack.
Below, close-ups of the devastation—maindeck in ruins, plates buckled, and rivets squeezed out by the heat.

from the Atlantic at speeds varying between four and seven and a half knots.

From the Russian convoy, from the convoys to Malta, from the Indian Ocean and from the borders of Australia, ships have come struggling home—ships which, but for fine seamanship and determination to hold on, must have been lost. When the *Kaimata* had an engine breakdown 500 miles from Melbourne, her Master, Captain J. E. Fenwick, O.B.E., in order to assist his engines, which had been mended well enough to do 35 revolutions, rigged hatch tarpaulins as square sails, two forward and two aft, with a trysail on the foreside of each mast ; and when the *Hororata*, torpedoed in the spring of 1943, sailed 240 miles to the Azores with a hole 32 feet by 28 feet above and below the water-line, it was the Master's inspiration and ingenuity which had helped to get the first patches swiftly applied and thus enabled her to reach Britain. Tree trunks were sawn down and fixed in the hold for support, and the great hole was patched partly with timber and partly with concrete.

Perhaps the largest British ship to be transformed from a wreck lying aground to a fine ship averaging $16\frac{1}{4}$ knots under her own steam is the liner *Georgic*, of 27,759 tons, built in 1932 at a cost of £2,000,000.

The *Georgic* was hit in an air raid on Suez harbour in 1941. Within 20 minutes the fire was beyond control and the Master, who had 120 civilian passengers on board, weighed anchor to berth the ship in shallow water. An hour and a half later she ran aground. Three boatloads of passengers got away in the normal manner, but others, owing to the spread of fire, had to be lowered by ropes from the forecastle.

The ship's decks were corrugated and twisted, and the interior damage was so great, turning her into little more than a hull, that a high military authority suggested using her as a pier at Ataka. Experts were flown from England. They decided she could be towed to India. After considerable patching up, the voyage began. To Port Sudan she was towed at six knots by two merchant ships, the *Clan Campbell* and the *City of Sydney*. It was a trying journey. After three days heavy weather sprang up and the aft wire connecting the *Georgic* with the *City of Sydney* parted. The *Clan Campbell* hung on, but the *Georgic* developed a list of 15 degrees. As soon as the weather abated, the *Georgic's* Master (Captain Greig) with Captain Manley, marine superintendent, and some engineers, went aboard and succeeded in starting up an emergency dynamo, which enabled pumps to be worked. The list was reduced to five degrees and the *City of Sydney* reconnected. But the *Georgic's* rudder was found to be jammed hard a-port. While work went on to free it, pumping continued till the list was down to three degrees. It was 12 days after leaving Suez that she gained harbour at Port Sudan. There she remained for a few weeks, the cement box (used in repair) being reinforced and the rudder bar freed. Two other vessels now took charge of her, the merchantman *Recorder* and the tug *St. Sampson*. Good progress was made for three days when, once more, the weather deteriorated and the tug *St. Sampson* was swamped, broke adrift and was lost after her crew had been rescued by the hospital ship *Dorsetshire*. Further help was signalled for and two days later the merchant ship *Haresfield* and the tug *Pauline Moller* arrived. The voyage was resumed and Karachi was reached within a month. Speed had averaged four knots. Crews were not aboard the *Georgic* all the time : they boarded her when needful, taking their meals with them.

In Karachi nine months' repair work was done under the *Georgic's* chief engineer, Mr. D. Horsburgh, who had with him 28 other engineers sent out from England, and 400 men, skilled and unskilled, engaged in Karachi. Early in 1943 she sailed from Bombay for Liverpool with 5,000 tons of pig iron. She voyaged independently and arrived safely, having seen nothing of the enemy. She had been away from England nearly two years.

THE GREAT CONVOY ROUTES

11. Ships in Company

Convoys in this war have been used from the beginning. On September 7th, 1939, the first outward-bound convoys across the Atlantic left our ports; others coming to the United Kingdom from Halifax, Jamaica, Gibraltar and Freetown sailed about a week later.

Organisation of convoys is the task of the Royal Navy. Vision had been shown; convoy staffs had been chosen for every major port in the world a good many months before the outbreak of war and they began to move towards their appointed stations when war was seen to be inevitable; most of them were in position when hostilities started.

They had their own difficulties; they did not yet know which countries would become allies, and which neutrals would be sympathetic or the reverse. Secrecy and security were imperative and not easy to achieve for ships had to be kept moving.

British Masters had been prepared. Numbers of them over the previous nine months had taken a week's course of lectures and demonstrations in convoy station-keeping, signals and signal books, the hazards they would meet from torpedoes, mines and raiders, and in their weapons of defence—guns, paravanes and so forth. It was something, if it was by no means everything. Messages had been arranged in advance which were broadcast by the Admiralty throughout the world, and ships at sea proceeded towards the assembly convoy ports. By September 27th, 1939, we had 14 large convoys at sea. There were exceptions, however. Fast ships—in general, ships making over 15 knots—sailed independently. Speed was, and is, looked on as a good defence against U-boats.

The enemy had U-boats and surface raiders in position, waiting for war, that they might attack swiftly. In the first week of war, 16 British, Allied or neutral ships were lost, totalling 80,000 tons; in the second week the number of ships lost was 17, the third week it fell to 10, and the fourth week to eight. Those were ships sunk by submarines, mines and raiders—80 per cent. by submarines. They were ships sailing out of convoy. *In* convoy only 12 vessels out of a

IN BATTLE ORDER, RANKED, SQUARED, DELIBERATE, THE CONVOY APPROACHES OUT OF THE CURVED DISTANCE

total of just over 5,900 had been lost by the end of 1939. During that period nine U-boats were destroyed.

Many problems arose in running the first convoys. On the one hand the Admiralty were sometimes difficult to convince that merchantmen do not always combine the discipline and precision of warships ; and on the other, some merchant crews and ships were a source of worry, straggling in convoy, belching smoke, throwing too much garbage overboard and showing lights. The need for putting fast and slow, new and old ships in the same convoy harassed both Admiralty and merchantmen. The third party concerned, the Ministry of War Transport, sometimes chafed at their inability to find an escort for every ship as soon as she was ready to sail, or at delays caused by suspected mine-laying in channels.

LIKE A CITY ON THE MARCH. AROUND ITS FORTY-FIVE SHIPS THE ESCORTS WEAVE THEIR NET OF PROTECTION

Nobody would pretend that perfection has been reached, but experience and improved co-ordination have smoothed most of the rough places. Masters have been encouraged to visit Whitehall and see for themselves how the protection of shipping is worked. Both when a convoy begins and ends, ship officers can discuss their problems with Naval Control Officers and Commodores.

Britain began this war, as she has begun all wars, short of convoy escort ships. From the start, we were short of destroyers, sloops and similar vessels. Nelson's remark that lack of frigates would be found written on his heart could have been echoed by any Admiral responsible for convoys in this war.

Troop convoys and operational convoys— to Malta, Russia, North Africa, among others —have usually been powerfully protected, but, although at the beginning of war every

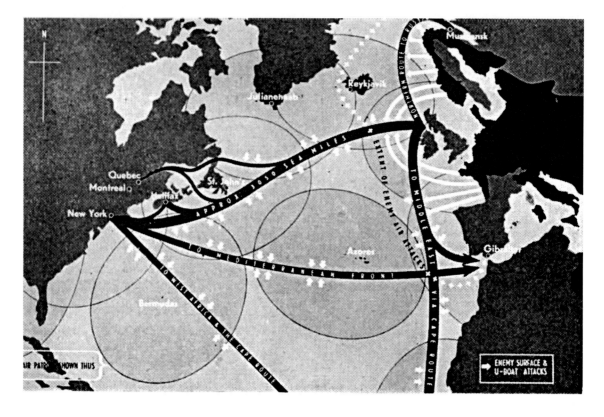

THE BATTLE OF THE ATLANTIC.

ocean convoy was guarded by heavy ships or armed merchant cruisers, it remains true that escorts of our cargo convoys have seldom —until recently—been as large as could be wished and often they have been lamentably small. Happily it was in Britain's favour that the Germans, in the war's early days, thought a convoy was a very dangerous thing to attack, and for about 12 months the menace of U-boats was far below what it became later. Indeed, the danger from enemy mines for a time was judged the greater, a danger largely overcome by the invention and use of degaussing early in 1940, and by other methods still secret.

Nor did the U-boats in the beginning go far afield. Many were close in round our coasts. Our convoys crossing the Atlantic were escorted half-way or thereabouts, and then dispersed to their various ports. At one

time an escort that sailed as far as 12½ degrees west was thought to be going far out. At a later date, ships went in convoy to 23 degrees west ; later still—after 18 months of war— they went the whole distance to America. Ships sailed in convoy, however, all the way across on the return journey, at a time when, outward, our escorts journeyed only half-way. The reason for the difference was that it is impossible to gather dispersed ships together and form them into a convoy in the middle of the ocean.

It is interesting to note now, in the sixth year of war, that aircraft protection from aircraft carriers was part of the first protection afforded to convoys in this war—doubly interesting at a time when escort carriers (the so-called " Woolworth carriers ") are doing such fine work in overcoming the U-boats. It is as though a wheel has come full circle.

Another early form of protection was that of the armed merchant cruiser. The *Rawalpindi* took on a pocket battleship as early as November 1939. The *Jervis Bay*, of glorious memory, was perhaps the most famous of them. She had nothing more powerful than six-inch guns when she turned to meet the German pocket battleship *Deutschland*, which shelled her convoy of 37 ships as dusk was falling on November 5th, 1940, several hundred miles west of Ireland. It is doubtful if the *Jervis Bay* ever got close enough to the raider for her fire to become effective before she was sunk, but her action, coupled with the dropping of smoke floats by the convoy, enabled 33 of the ships to disperse and escape. Captain E. S. F. Fegen, R.N., of the *Jervis Bay* was posthumously awarded the V.C.

Ships' Masters remember the armed merchant cruisers as ships which did valiant work against odds ; they would sometimes zigzag behind the convoy by day and in front of it at night ; they were unwieldy, and against U-boats could do little, but they were admirable watchdogs and, as did the *Jervis Bay*, they could make the enemy, on occasion, diffident or cautious. The period when they were of greatest service was that when Britain was hardest pressed.

The fall of France had, among other results, two that were vital to convoys ; it gave the enemy the secret of our Asdic apparatus for detecting submarines (knowledge they had lacked and now gained from Vichy France), and it caused many escort ships to be moved to even more vital duties, so that Britain passed through a time when a cargo convoy might sail forth with nothing more powerful than a sloop and a trawler to guard it. One convoy, the record tells, was guarded by the Duke of Westminster's yacht. Merchant Masters speak drily but not without humour of the days when escorts (in their phrase) were things you " read about in books " ; one Master speaks of 40 ships going out in charge of a motor-boat which accompanied them 200 miles and then blessed them and said adieu ; a second recalls standing on his bridge in mid-Atlantic, one of 30 ships, when their escort hove in sight. His first officer, a Cockney, exclaimed, " Blimey ! Look what they've sent us—a lifeboat and a raft ! " What had come to guard them was in fact a corvette and a trawler. *Punch* had a cartoon showing an enormous vessel and, alongside it, a cockle of a craft. An officer on the giant is looking overboard and remarking, " We're all right—our escort's arrived ! " But the truth behind that cartoon is a measure of what Britain's ships and men have done. Like the soldiers, they have won through against long odds. The Royal Navy was ill provided and did its best. The gift by the United States of 50 old destroyers was a rich asset, but it did not fill the gap.

In the autumn of 1940 the German U-boats sailed farther west ; it was not that they were getting larger, but their endurance was rising. To-day some are undoubtedly supplied with fuel, food and ammunition at sea. Sinkings occurred farther west in the Atlantic, from 15 degrees to 20 degrees west. Our seamen, with their blunt, grim tongues, christened that stretch " the Graveyard ". We began to use the waters of the North Atlantic, dangerous from storms and icebergs as they were ; Masters who had hated these waters became glad to go there.

Not only were the submarines increasing in range but in number also. By the spring of 1942 over 250 of them were in the Atlantic at one and the same time. Whereas in the last war U-boats rarely did their work in more than ones or twos, they now hunted in packs of a dozen, of even 20 or 25. As early as mid-1940 it was noticed that more than one U-boat would converge on a convoy and thenceforward the number steadily increased. Moreover, there was a period when this U-boat activity at its greatest was coupled with attacks from the air ; long-range Focke-Wulf Condors searched the seas for the ship sailing alone or for the straggler, even for the convoy itself. The reply to that was, in part, the C.A.M. ship—a cargo ship with a catapulted aircraft. These vessels were first used in May 1941, and by the middle of 1942 the C.A.M. ships and the escort carriers with fighter aircraft and Coastal Command, R.A.F., had virtually put an end to the Focke-Wulfs' ocean activities. The merchantmen, too, were now better armed : it was in 1941 that army and naval gunners first went aboard cargo ships to use the new armament, and Masters began to feel they commanded a small warship.

It was in 1941 also that the rescue ships were created to sail with convoys, and the Royal Navy corvettes joined the battle. While the enemy on their part sent U-boats farther afield—to the Caribbean Sea, to the North and South Atlantic, so that from time to time the waters off Freetown were highly dangerous—we on our side steadily increased detective and protective devices (radio-location for one, and several not yet to be disclosed) and built up the numbers and types of escort ships, until we have close escorts and escorts working farther off, the latter up to the size of capital ships. Nor are naval ships the only means of protection. Guard from the air has steadily increased ; it is this lengthening guard, from long-range aircraft and aircraft flown from escort carriers, which has bridged the mid-Atlantic gulf so that, in reasonable flying weather, there is hardly any part of our Atlantic routes to-day on which a U-boat can raise its head with complete safety.

This air protection which has made our merchant seamen air-minded, is given to single ships also when these are within range. The guard over single ships sailing the oceans alone is as thoroughly kept by the Admiralty as its watch over convoys. A fast ship coming from Australia or America is under constant surveillance ; its route may be changed, on instructions by wireless, half a dozen times if the presence of U-boats or raiders or foul weather makes that desirable. But if the route looks constantly good it may not be changed at all.

Evasive routeing for convoys and for single ships is a day and night task both at the Admiralty and for the staffs under naval Commanders-in-Chief in various parts of the world. Choice of route and ships' protection is to-day the joint responsibility of the Royal Navy and the United States Navy. The Admiralty controls the North Atlantic in detail and frames the policy for the rest of the Atlantic and the Indian Ocean, while the more distant seas are controlled by the Commanders-in-Chief concerned. The American Navy controls the Western Atlantic and Pacific Oceans. Close co-operation and exchange of ideas go on without pause.

Convoys have drawbacks that are not disputed. Yet the evidence in their favour is conclusive. From the moment they were begun in the last war the U-boat danger shrank. Convoys saved us. From the time in this war when escorts by sea and air became reasonably adequate the U-boat danger again diminished. The Germans, when this war started, looked on a convoy as something perilous to the attacker ; their early fears are proving well founded.

---

12. "They Stand Towards the West"

THE sun is setting, throwing its pale light across the water when the ships, one by one, pick themselves up from among those that remain and move off almost imperceptibly. Half an hour earlier wisps of steam appeared at their bows, thrown off by windlasses as they weighed anchor, and now from the smoke-stacks thin black or grey columns begin to rise. A man can hardly watch them going without being stirred. There is the 10,000-ton tramp that has been four times to

FIVE HOURS OUT. Before them lie 3,000 miles of Atlantic storms and enemy attack. These patient ships are the slender bridges that link the armed base of Britain with the arsenal of the New World.

Russia by the Northern route—still fitted like a Shackleton Expedition ship ; there is the ancient ship, a foreign prize, brought to the Clyde from Gibraltar by a chief officer of 27, whose own ship had been disabled in the Malta convoy. This old ship had boilers which blew out on small provocation and a radio set that threatened to go on fire if anyone approached it, and it was known that if the engines once stopped they would never start again ; but she has been overhauled and patched and made shipshape in the past six months, and although she has essayed to go to America once before and failed, she is making the attempt again to-night. Others are less picturesque but have seen perhaps sterner work, crossing and recrossing those broad, tempestuous and dangerous seas—the tankers, cargo liners, tramps, whalers, Liberty

ships ; and there are one or two Empire ships off on their first voyage, recruits among the veterans.

An hour or two before sailing time, a former sea captain now representing the Ministry of War Transport has made a final call on every ship, finding out if the Master has all he wants, and whether his crew are all on board. He may have found a fireman short here, a fourth engineer there ; he may discover an engineer struggling with only partial success to get oil through to his furnaces. The missing men are found ; experts are rushed out to the ship's furnaces, that the convoy may sail intact. It was in such circumstances that a Master who was signalled to raise heaven and earth to get started, replied by Aldis lamp : " Have raised heaven and earth ; am now raising hell ! "

SWELL   FOG

Presently they are gone. At the appointed rendezvous at sea they will be joined by ships from other ports, till, the convoy complete, and the naval escort shepherding them, they all stand towards the west.

Although submarine attacks varied, the spring weather of 1943 was steadily atrocious, fitting successor to a winter that had damaged the bridges of liners on several occasions. There are Commodores and Masters who have sailed in convoys to Murmansk and Archangel and found the North Atlantic worse. Ships can drive through ice in the Davis Strait for days on end, davits can be frozen up and rafts frozen to decks. Icebergs in the North Atlantic were at one time in this war held to offer more dangers than submarines ; fogs or even snow-squalls can be thick as a hedge for hours or days on end. In very heavy weather, seas of 40 or 50 feet are encountered.

The convoy in its approved formation, which may be altered as circumstances change, or attacks are encountered, steams on. The individual Master, although he may know little or nothing of the whereabouts of U-boats, has even in quiet hours much to do. He must keep his station, maintain the number of revolutions on his engines (or rather his engineers must) that will preserve his allotted cables' lengths from the ship ahead. He must watch for the Commodore's signals by flag or Aldis lamp, and be ready to alter course by zigzag or otherwise. The most important signals must be as familiar to him as the face of his chief officer. In fog or wretched visibility he must keep station by sound. Moreover, although his training was for peace, he is now commanding a ship well armed for its defence, and carrying seven to ten (or even 20 or more) naval and maritime gunners using an armament that includes a 4.7 anti-submarine gun, Oerlikon 20 mm. guns, machine-guns, and various rockets and projectors. He finds himself working in closest co-operation with the Royal Navy, accustomed to a destroyer or corvette dashing alongside, perhaps asking him through the loud hailer to " turn up the wick, old man", if he is lagging a trifle, or standing by him if he gets into trouble through engine failure or more serious

96

STORM

disaster. A North Atlantic convoy is a joint operation in the truest sense.

Most, but not all, U-boat attacks are now made at night, and by submarines on the surface, so that U-boats have been once or twice described as "surface ships that can submerge". A Master sailing in a convoy of many columns spread over miles of sea can be ignorant of what happens, in pitch darkness, on the far wing. He may hear a dull thud as a torpedo strikes, or he may not; it depends on the direction of wind. If he is looking by chance in the right direction, he may see a column of water shoot up into the night, or he may see the flash of explosion. But none of this is certain.

A Master who sailed during March said: " We had three days of fog, followed by days of squalls of snow and rain. At times the cabins were knee-deep in sea-water. We ran before the gale—weather as thick as a hedge. I said, ' There'll be some fun if somebody heaves to and we don't see 'em', and soon after the ship ahead did: we saw her two red lights and went hard a-starboard and just missed her; had to go beam on to the sea to do it. This was about midnight, a thick, overcast night, black. The convoy was flattened out, partly dispersed, and we signalled some of the ships with Aldis to get 'em back. We hadn't quite reached the middle of the Atlantic then.

" Next night there was a heavy swell. I was sitting down for a couple of minutes about eight o'clock when the third officer knocked at my door and said: 'A ship's just been torpedoed'. I went up on to the bridge. We'd some American Liberty ships in the convoy. I said: ' I'll bet they're hoping the lady-welders have made a good job of those ships'. A ship at the head of the third column had got it, but it looked as though a corvette was alongside her.

" We just kept plugging on. I was a rear ship so I signalled the Commodore: ' Reference Article so-and-so, am I to act as rescue ship without any further signal from you?' He replied ' Yes '. I then said to my crew: ' If anything further is hit, we turn back'. We all felt better then—cheered up at the idea of doing something constructive. We'd had some good practice in New York harbour moving the ship about in snow and bad weather with ships dragging—good training for moving about in the convoy. It was about 3 a.m. when we saw a flash and heard a bit of banging on the other wing. Then the leader of our wing went up with a hell of a wallop ; two great columns of water rose about 200 feet in the air. I said : ' All hands on deck'.

" A torpedo came right across the convoy and missed our stern by about 30 feet. Next, a whaler factory ship went up close by. Our radio officer thought we ourselves were hit—you can't always tell for a minute or two. Anyhow, we were all right and we turned left to go to the whaler. Fellows were floating about in the water—the red lights on their lifejackets were like a carpet of red fireflies in the water : some men were whistling quite chirpily and others were shouting like mad. We steamed gently and then drifted among them. At first, some of them thought we were a derelict and tried to get away from us. We had ropes with bowlines, and we would drop a bowline over a man, and five or six of my men would haul him up. It was dark, but the men made darker blobs in the water, and the whaler's ammunition magazine kept going off, giving us a bit of light ; I saw one rocket shoot right up into the sky and coloured tracer was going up, too. A ship which was on fire several cables' lengths off lit things up a bit, too. We were four hours picking chaps up— we picked up 146 altogether. We sailed within 30 feet of the American ship. She was like a ghost ship, low in the water for'ard and with a torch left burning on her deck."

THE EYE OF THE ENEMY. This photograph, taken inside a German submarine, shows a convoy seen through the sights of the periscope. The U-boat is shadowing the convoy, waiting for the straggler, watching for the opening.

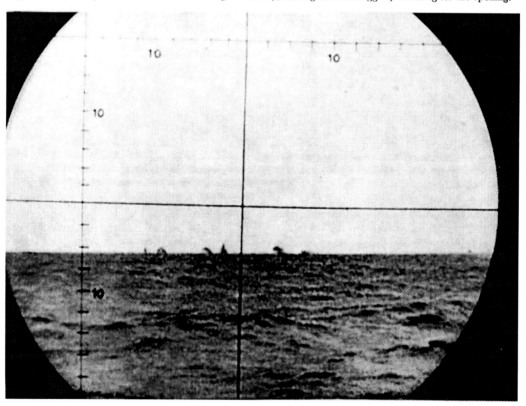

During this time the destroyers and corvettes will have been hurrying to and fro like hounds, nosing out the enemy, endeavouring to ram, and depth-charging wherever a U-boat is known to have dived. In these night fights, which sometimes tax the crews' stamina for three, four, five or up to eight successive nights, and in which the enemy may lose as many U-boats as we lose cargo ships, the merchantmen cannot often take an active part. Frequently they can do little more than keep ploughing steadily on, trusting to God, good fortune and the Royal Navy.

However, on occasion the cargo ships have sunk the enemy, too. This extract is from what Captain J. T. Hair, of the m.v. *Cromarty* wrote at sea in September 1941 : " At approximately 9.15 p.m., with three corvettes ranged somewhere slightly ahead of the convoy, the second attack opened. It appeared to be made by several submarines ranged in two blocks, one on either side and forward of the convoy, firing their torpedoes diagonally. The action started with two loud detonations from the direction of the port wing columns, followed by white rockets and red flares. Almost immediately the attack developed ahead and on the starboard side ; explosions, clouds of smoke, white rockets and red flares appeared from various parts of the convoy, which began to increase speed and disperse. It was then that two torpedoes passed across our bows at a distance of about six feet and scored a hit on a ship in the next column. A large explosion and cloud of smoke came from the direction of the Commodore's ship.

THE EYE OF THE FRIEND. In this photograph, taken from an American Liberator, three enemy submarines cut flurries of spray as they turn to avoid the bombs of Coastal Command aircraft. All were destroyed.

" As we were the leading ship of the starboard wing column, we increased speed, altering course to starboard and zigzagging as we got clear of the main body of the convoy. In company with us on our port side was a tanker, and on our starboard side was a freighter. By 11.30 p.m. the tanker had drawn ahead of us and the freighter had gone away to starboard. It was then that the tanker was hit by a torpedo and seemed to turn towards us and we veered off sharply to starboard to avoid collision. As we were swinging and parallel with the tanker, a submarine was sighted between us and the blaze, showing all foredeck to after-part of the conning-tower. Fire was opened with our Hotchkiss gun to give gunners aft a line of direction, and the order to open fire was given to the 4-inch gun crew, who fired seven rounds, the third and fourth of which were hits. The submarine was seen to disappear stern first, her bows coming up as she sank. During the firing my vessel hit something along the starboard side. This jar and scrape were distinctly heard and felt both on deck and down in the engine-room, the vessel giving a slight lurch to port. In all probability we hit the submarine that torpedoed the tanker. We drew away from the zone without further incident."

When harbour is safely reached, the Master's chief anxiety is ended. But some worries remain. A ship's captain, who has done 53 years at sea and is still sailing, said, admittedly with some irony—for it is seldom that a Master takes his clothes off during convoy, and rare are the days when he gets more than a few hours' broken sleep—" Being at sea is easy. Once in port, the troubles come, what with paying the men, getting repairs done, seeing naval and transport authorities, dealing with documents, papers, having guns and ammunition seen to, and the rest of it". But it is in port, too, that the captains, officers and crews of the various ships forgather like a small army withdrawn from battle, to take a drink on the job accomplished, growl and indulge in badinage.

The year 1943 saw the turn in the Battle of the Atlantic. The Admiralty and R.A.F. were able to say that complete shore to shore air cover had been provided in the Atlantic by Fleet aircraft from escort carriers in co-operation with land-based aircraft of Coastal Command and of U.S.A. and Canada, and that a convoy had sailed free from attack although strong forces of U-boats were near it. In other words, the mid-Atlantic gap of several hundred miles, in which U-boats had hitherto been free from air attack, was now being closed.

The results were immediate. Thenceforward the U-boat, the traditional hunter, became himself the prey. During May, June, and July, over 90 were sent to the bottom. The reinforcements became cautious, and in August hardly any attempt was made to attack our convoys in the North Atlantic ; gunners grew bored ; voyages were serene. In September, however, a new outbreak occurred ; a pack of at least fifteen submarines attacked a westbound convoy for four and a half days. Three escort ships were lost and some merchantmen, but the U-boats themselves suffered as much or more. In October the U-boats introduced new weapons and new tactics, and the battle both of seamen and the scientists behind them was vigorous.

But the course of the battle was in no doubt. Month by month we were destroying more U-boats than they were sinking merchantmen. In November, when we began to base aircraft on the Azores, fewer merchant ships were lost to U-boats than in any month since May 1940, despite the enemy's use of long-range aircraft to help concentrate his submarines. Throughout 1943 our tonnage lost to U-boats was only 40 per cent. of that of the year before, and only a fourth of that tonnage was sunk during the second half of the year.

The year 1944 opened with U-boats showing extreme caution ; but caution failed to save them if they attacked. Their vulnerability and their losses continued steadily higher than that of merchantmen. In March, submarine strength was described in the joint

THE OTHER SIDE. Like wheeling birds that foreshadow the presence of land, U.S. naval aircraft fly out to welcome the incoming convoy and shepherd it into harbour.

statement of Mr. Roosevelt and Mr. Churchill as " remaining considerable and calling for powerful efforts ". Those powerful efforts did their work, for in May 1944 the shipping losses were the lowest for the whole war. A convoy of over 40 ships, including 21 tankers, had only two brief U-boat alarms while sailing from America to England early in May, and a 20,000-ton troopship in the convoy could say that this was her first U-boat alarm for two years.

During June, the U-boats in the Atlantic apparently concentrated to the west of the Allied invasion fleets. Other U-boats, in substantial numbers, attempted to pass up-Channel from their bases in Norway and France. Both enemy moves were frustrated. Shipping losses were almost as light in June as in May, and of the vast concourse of ships moving across the Channel to Normandy and along the coast to build up the forces engaged in the liberation of Europe only one merchant vessel was lost as the possible result of U-boat action—and in that case it is not certain that a U-boat was responsible.

For many months America's great armies had been reaching Britain not without discomfort in travel conditions—crowded ships and an intractable sea made sure of that—but with virtually perfect safety. That was the yardstick of our triumph. The worst in the North Atlantic was long since over.

GERMAN TORPEDO-BOMBERS SWIRL ABOVE THE BARENTS SEA AS THE CONVOY FIGHTS ITS WAY TO RUSSIA.

13. The Route to Russia

OUR convoys to Russia by the northern route to Murmansk and Archangel hold a most honourable place in the history of this war. They have taken supplies from Britain, America and Canada at a time when the need has been crucial, and they have done it by facing, as no other convoys have quite faced, the triple perils of surface raiders from battleships downwards, of U-boats in strength, and of bombers and torpedo-bombers.

The main part of the German fleet was concentrated in the Northern Fjords, and about 350 of the enemy's most powerful aircraft were used solely to intercept our ships. Moreover, the physical ordeal during winter has been severe. To be sunk in the Arctic means that even though men are saved they often lose limbs from frostbite. On this route a few individual Masters, deck officers, engineers and men have voyaged three or four times.

The first Russian convoy sailed in August 1941. It consisted of six British tramp steamers, subsequently joined by a Soviet vessel. The convoy arrived at Archangel in September, without being attacked *en route*, and delivered 64 fighter aircraft, 32 special vehicles and over 15,000 tons of mixed military cargo. Other convoys followed and, by the close of 1941, 572 tanks, 799 fighter

BLACK SMOKE PILLARING FROM A TORPEDOED SHIP JOINS THE GREY SEA TO A LEADEN ROOF OF CLOUDS.

aircraft, 1,404 vehicles and nearly 100,000 tons of other military cargo had been shipped —all of it without loss. Thirty-six British cargo ships and seven Russian had done the work. As time went on, convoys began to include ships of many Allied nations. American ships with American crews became steadily more numerous, but there were Dutch, Norwegian and Polish, in addition to our own.

The voyage is usually one of some 2,500 miles. At the height of summer it is made in almost constant daylight, apart from an hour or two of gloaming or dusk, and in the depth of winter the situation is reversed—the conditions are of constant night broken only by an hour or two's grey daylight. But these extreme conditions are arrived at through weeks of change. A ship's captain put it thus: "From February onwards it is lighting up quickly. At the end of January there are four hours' daylight, end of February eight hours' daylight, end of April 20 hours', and July and August virtually 24 hours' daylight, with sun all the time, which works along the horizon. From April to August there's no really bad weather; conditions are ideal for enemy day attack. Winter starts in September, and from October to the end of December there's a lot of fog and heavy snowstorms but not much wind. From the end of December you may get gales of hurricane strength which can last five days, but between the gales the weather may be flat. In the winds, a big short sea is built up—seldom more than

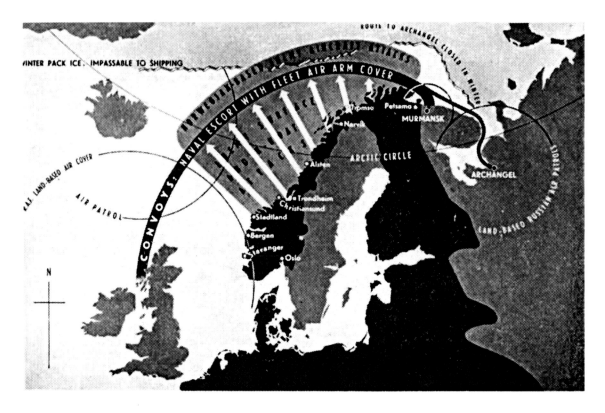

THE NORTHERN ROUTE TO RUSSIA.

15 feet, even in bad weather, for the seas are comparatively shallow—but in those big short seas the ship rolls like hell".

Murmansk is ice-free. Not so Archangel. On the voyage to both ports during winter, floating bergs and floes are encountered and, indeed, small floating seas of ice many square miles in extent : but, sailing to Archangel, it is in the Strait of Gorlo leading into the White Sea that real difficulty arises. Through this strait, some 40 miles in width, the tide runs in and out swiftly, and rises and falls 18 to 25 feet. Ice begins to form early in November, and from mid-December to May 20th or so a tramp steamer cannot sail through the strait except behind the ice-breaker. For 100 to 150 miles the ice-breaker forces her bows through ice a yard thick, the ship riding on the ice and then crashing

through, the stern of the ship riding in free water. The tramp ships must keep close on the breaker's heels or ice may freeze up between the two and the breaker have to retrace her steps. For ice to freeze-in swiftly behind the tramp ships, closing up the narrow sea-lane once more, as soon as the convoy has passed, is common enough. Occasionally a ship has been locked in the ice for a lengthy period. One or two have remained at Archangel for as long as seven months.

Icing can vary a good deal. A captain who returned from Archangel in the winter of 1941 said it took him 16 days to move 70 miles, and that every night his men were able to leave the ship and walk across the ice to neighbouring ships. They turned the propeller every ten minutes to keep it free from ice. On the other hand, a Master describing a later voyage to Russia said that his ship got very little ice on her, but the small naval escorts looked like sugar boats, as though they had sailed off a cake.

This voyage into the White Sea in winter is being performed by our merchant seamen for the first time in history. Before the war Narvik was looked on as being far north. The northern route to Russia, however, has frequently taken our cargo vessels to latitude 76 degrees, within 750 miles of the North Pole and in temperatures registering from 45 to 80 degrees of frost. They have reached the journey's end, sometimes carrying a load of 50 to 150 tons of ice—ice encrusting the ship's hull, shrouds coated with ice that has become streamlined, icicles hanging thick as a man's arm from the rigging, and a casing of ice round the winches, although those winches have probably been kept turning without pause since Iceland was left behind to ensure their working in Russian ports. Even inside the ship, portholes can be frozen solid and ice on interior walls sparkle " like a ballroom ", as a Master put it.

To meet these unexampled sailing conditions our ships and men are specially equipped. Ships' propellers are made of cast-steel. In oil-burning vessels a light grade of fuel oil is used and this is heated by steam coils so that it flows freely. The general heating installations are, roughly, doubled—extra stoves and pipes fitted, all exposed pipes insulated, and cabin roofs sheathed with asbestos to prevent excess condensation from steel decks. Compasses tend to be troublesome, to " dip to the Pole " and to be affected by the concentration of ore at Narvik. On key ships, therefore, such as the Commodore's, gyro compasses are fitted. The bridge and important upper structures are usually insulated by a casing of woollen fabric, and in addition there are thick plastic slabs as armour against bomb splinters and bullets. Ships develop a stodgy, robot-like appearance.

Crews undergo a special medical examination. Hooded Duffle coats are issued, lined with lamb's wool and padded round the skirt, together with an extra hood which has only slits for eyes and mouth : underclothing has the thickness of a man's white sweater, and so have the two pairs of long socks for the leather sea-boots. Fur-lined mittens have a separate thumb and separate first finger.

Less imagination is required, perhaps, to picture life on deck than life below, for here engineers, greasers, firemen and the rest enjoy more warmth but can experience more tension. When the outside world, unseen and mostly unknown, is brought to you only by the din, explosions and gunfire, a wide vision can be a drawback, and an engineer may be glad to find " something to tinker at ", as they say, something to keep the nose down and the mind engrossed. The chief engineer of the tramp ship *Empire Baffin* certainly had enough to occupy him. Three days from Russia, at the height of an attack, the engines gave what is called " a nasty kick ", and when he went down to the engine-room the place was full of smoke, soot and steam. The greaser on watch, who had been in the tunnel, reported that all the tunnel bearings were broken. The chief engineer went down the tunnel himself and found that this was true and there were no means of lubricating those bearings. He reported to the captain, however, that he believed he could make repairs and carry on. Now there is no means of getting out of the tunnel except by a long climb out of the trunk escape, and it was the chief engineer who, alone, fitted a temporary method of lubricating the bearings and for three days and nights, during constant enemy attacks, oiled those bearings every hour. This also he did alone. (The tunnel which contains the propeller shaft runs along the bottom of the ship from the engine-room aft and is some 112 feet in length and high enough for a man to walk through. The trunk escape is at the after end with a ladder about 35 feet high. Six bearings would need greasing by hand every hour.)

A chief engineer, giving temperatures

below decks in Murmansk, said it was 60 degrees in the stokehold and 80 in the engine-room ; that was comfortable, but there were a lot of cold draughts to be kept out. The Arab firemen, he said, stoked during the voyage wearing extra jerseys and a leather jerkin and sometimes with their lifejackets on. He thought it was better in some ways to be below during an action, for you know less what is going on.

To Russia we take, as a typical ship's cargo, tanks and aircraft almost as a matter of course, but also motor-cycles, ammunition, butter, canned meat, camouflage nets, dried eggs, ether, flour, lard (a lot of lard has been carried), machinery of various sorts, torpedoes, Red Cross stores, rope, X-ray units and R.A.F. lighthouses. Seventy to eighty major items are normally carried in a convoy. On the return voyage, ships bring mainly lumber, apatite (a fertiliser), potash, chrome ore, and some skins.

The stay in Murmansk Harbour has usually been enlivened by bombing, for the nearest enemy airfield at Petsamo is only 70 miles distant. A chief engineer, describing one convoy, said : " The air raid alarms became so frequent that the bell rang nearly all the time until at last we took no notice of it. The Germans came over in threes and fours : we were all right by day because our ships can look after themselves quite well, but night wasn't so good. But we didn't get hit, though another ship did. We began to say bad weather was good, and good weather bad. We had the banquet on a cloudy night ".

It has been a common practice at Murmansk for German fighter bombers to trail behind Russian bombers, following them in, and then suddenly to dive on to our ships. The enemy have come with regularity over the hill not far from the harbour and our ship's gunners have learned to sit with their guns trained on that hill, waiting for them to appear.

On the more recent convoys an extra deck officer has been carried to lighten watch-keeping, and the number of naval and maritime gunners raised to 20 or 22. A British tramp steamer to Russia—and they are mostly tramp ships which make the voyage—carries a 4-inch gun, a 12-pounder, a Bofors, six Oerlikons, two pom-poms, eight parachute rockets, two machine-guns and a Ross rifle. Her Master may refer to her proudly and with some justification as " a young light cruiser ". Some convoys have had the benefit of aircraft flown from a British naval carrier, or catapulted from a British ship ; and when convoys near the Russian ports Russian fighters have on many an occasion given protection.

The first convoys on the northern route, as stated earlier, got through without loss. Some convoys were attacked, mainly by a few enemy destroyers (as in December 1941), but without success. Enemy air attack had not yet begun on the northern route— possibly airfields were not ready ; it seems doubtful also if the enemy was fully awake to the volume of supplies that were being sent. At all events, not till the spring of 1942, when daylight had lengthened and weather improved, did attacks develop increasing weight.

It was in March that the first outward-bound ship was lost. Captain S. M. Lamont, O.B.E., of the tramp ship *Temple Arch*, who sailed about that time, noted that the *Tirpitz* came out and threatened them, but returned to port on being attacked by the Fleet Air Arm. The following convoy, he adds, was attacked by destroyers as well as submarines, in a fight when the cruiser *Trinidad* was damaged. On the homeward passage air attacks and submarine attacks were frequent.

This was the beginning of what may be called the middle period of the Russian convoys, during which attacks grew in violence, coming from bombers, U-boats and, more rarely, from surface craft. Merchant ships' crews have noticed that they are attacked more often when outward than homeward bound, especially from the air.

Often enough they have had to break through a line of U-boats to get back to Britain.

A tramp ship's Master who has made four round voyages in the same ship may be quoted : " From 700 miles off the North Cape onwards, the ships are usually dogged by a Focke-Wulf aircraft which flies to and fro ahead, or goes round and round the convoy, as though it were a Catalina escorting you, signalling to U-boats, and occasionally dropping flares. This aircraft is relieved regularly at 9 a.m. and 1 p.m".

" In December 1941", continues the Master quoted above, " I was Commodore of a convoy when, two days from Iceland, we were attacked by three German destroyers. I scattered the convoy and night saved us. Later on, again to avoid the destroyers, I took the ships into the ice—about four miles

NORTHERN RESCUE. The men waiting their turn to climb to safety are on a sinking ship. Another has come to their rescue, drawn dangerously alongside. The lives of seamen depend on the speed of their rescue. Men overboard do not last long in Arctic waters.

in, where we remained seven or eight hours. Owing to their thin plates, the destroyers couldn't follow us." This tactic of sailing into the ice has been followed several times. Another Master who sailed on a different occasion into an icefield 20 miles by 10, with open water in its middle, said he did it at a time when five heavy German destroyers were being beaten off by five of the old United States destroyers manned by the Royal Navy. To break into the ice it was necessary to drive as gently as possible to the edge of the crust and then sail full steam ahead. It took ten minutes to drive through ; the ice stood about two feet above the water. Eighteen ships followed him and they sailed round in the hole, which was three or four miles across, while the action was fought outside.

The Master first quoted proceeds : " My next convoy was in April 1942, the weather still very cold. We were attacked by seven German destroyers, but four of ours— actually old United States destroyers—kept them off. The firing lasted about 2½ hours and spray from some of the shells fell on deck. The tale about spray freezing as it falls is all rot, in my experience. Three days later we were attacked by eight U-boats, and the Commodore and his ship were lost. This was about 10.30 a.m. The Commodore was last seen in the water with a stump of cigar in his mouth, waving us on. The attack had come from quarter and bows. Two torpedoes came past our bow and two past our stern. I had 63 men on deck at the time—all the crew and gunners. Only two engineers and three stokers were down below.

" Each man has a whistle and he blows it when he sees a torpedo. The torpedo is actually travelling 50 yards ahead of its wash, so if the wash hits the ship you know the torpedo is safely past. A man who doesn't know that may lose his nerve.

" I put the helm hard a-port and squeezed her through between the torpedoes. This ship will do a full circle in four minutes ; if on the swing, she'll turn with the swing enough to dodge in about 30 seconds ; if against the swing, one and a half minutes." The German method, he said, as he has seen it, appears to be to fire what is called a " Browning shot " (possibly derived from the old term of browning a covey of partridges, i.e., aiming at none in particular) from ahead and the flanks of the convoy, each submarine firing two or more torpedoes. Having done this, the U-boats withdraw out of range and lie in wait, so far as possible, for the convoy to reach them once more. On this occasion the U-boat battle went on for four days.

Another Master, asked to picture the scene in action said : " One would hear six short blasts on a siren. That meant torpedoes. Two blasts would be a warning from a ship that she was going to swing, perhaps out of control. The Commodore would give a long blast to draw our attention. During an air attack you might well see eight separate fights going on between ships and aircraft". In his opinion, the air is colder than the sea and he advised his men, if they found themselves in the water, not to climb out on to a raft but to lash themselves to the raft with the fathom of line tied to the lifejacket, and remain in the sea until picked up by a ship.

By the end of July 1944, this doughty work had resulted in the dispatch from the United Kingdom to North Russian ports of 3,480 tanks, 3,200 aircraft, 7,800 vehicles of all descriptions, and over 500,000 tons of stores.

The Master first quoted said : " During my third voyage to Russia a great number of torpedo bombers—I should say close on a hundred—attacked over several days and we watched the cruiser *Scylla* shoot down 35 of them. I congratulated the Admiral and he replied, ' Just like grouse shooting'. My own ship brought down nine. I got a message : ' Proud to have sailed with you. Courage undaunted '. It was a nice, calm day, light airs, fine and clear. Those bombers came in only 20 feet above the water". Later they were trying the method of rising and falling like porpoises—" and between the lines of ships. The first time they attacked we got two, and one of my naval gunners kept on firing his Oerlikon when blood was pouring off the heel of his boot from a wound. The next day at 1 p.m. they came again, 25 this time, and none got away. My ship shot down seven. H.M.S. *Jason* signalled ' Good shooting. I wish I had your guns'. I replied ' Thanks. I wish I had your speed '. The seven we shot down were only about a cable's length off—that's 200 yards. They thought it was a piece of pie once they'd got past the escort. Of course, a lot never got as far as us. On the day after, there was dense fog—we pray for fog—and the day following, a snowstorm. Near the Strait of Gorlo, 14 torpedo bombers attacked us, but the Commodore signalled me : ' They don't seem to have as much guts as before', for the bombers had dropped their torpedoes two miles away. I was usually the vice-Commodore on my trips". He smiled drily. " I was always the blushing bridesmaid but never the blushing bride."

Continuing, the Master said that on his fourth Russian convoy Junkers bombed from high altitude while submarines surfaced and fired their torpedoes. The aircraft also dropped mines ahead and circular torpedoes (torpedoes that describe an arc or circle in the water) and course had to be altered. Three men on his ship were wounded, he added. " The rescue ship came alongside, within a foot of me, and didn't touch me. I was going normal speed at the time. The wounded were helped to the rail, and the rescue ship, steaming alongside, lifted them over the rail and then sheered off. You'd never think of doing it in peace time, and you wouldn't believe it unless you saw it."

On the outward journey in January, he continued, they were attacked only once, when about 150 miles from the Norwegian coast. Three torpedo bombers came in at water level but all three were shot down ; the first stood almost on its tail with a spurt of flame issuing from it, then turned over, dived into the water and drifted past with a piece of wing protruding and its rubber boat

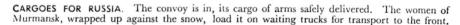

CARGOES FOR RUSSIA. The convoy is in, its cargo of arms safely delivered. The women of Murmansk, wrapped up against the snow, load it on waiting trucks for transport to the front.

inflated and sailing on the water, but empty. The second broke in two, and the third was hit by at least three tramp steamers' guns. " You could fairly see the red tracer plugging into those bombers, yet for some time they continued to come on." On the return voyage, 12 aircraft came in at 3,000 feet and dropped eight bombs in the centre of the convoy, but all missed. He said : " We at the head of the line (he had the Commodore aboard) could look round and see our ships steadily plodding on like soldiers on parade, never deviating, doing their seven or eight knots, and when the columns of water had subsided—you don't hear anything, you merely see the spouts of water—there the ships still were, plodding serenely on".

The amount of rest and sleep men get when sailing this route differs with the job to be done, with varying responsibility, and temperament. But it is clear that men of middle age have performed remarkable feats. Of the three Masters quoted, the first said : " There was a period of two months and 25 days when I never took all my clothes off— I tried to wash my feet and change my socks every other day. I don't think I slept undisturbed during that period for more than one and a half hours at a stretch. I used to sit with my feet up against the book-case—you can see the marks on it ".

It should not be supposed that because little has been said concerning the losses on this route they have always been light. At times they have been heavy. When the sea is " alive with torpedoes", as one ship's officer described it, each of 25 torpedo bombers having dropped three, it would be miraculous if all ships escaped hits. It was observed in September 1942 that a ship, the *Dan-y-Bryn* had six torpedoes running more or less parallel to her after making her 45 degrees turn. Only sound seamanship and quick wits saved her. In loss of life, as of ships, two convoys have seldom been alike. In all, hundreds of survivors, among them women and children, have been taken aboard other vessels. Of 85 rescued on one occasion, eight were women and 11 were children—three of them babies less than a year old.

In the words of Mr. Maisky, the former Soviet Ambassador to Britain, spoken when presenting decorations to British seamen on behalf of his Government, the Russian convoys have been magnificent exploits. " They are ", he said, " a Northern saga of heroism, bravery and endurance, and the price had to be paid. This saga will live for ever not only in the hearts of your people, but also in the hearts of the Soviet people, who rightly see in it one of the most striking expressions of collaboration between the Allied Nations".

Note.—The author desires to acknowledge with grateful thanks the help he received when gathering information for this chapter from Captain Hugh MacLeod, D.S.C., of the *Dan-y-Bryn*, Captain W. H. Lawrence, C.B.E., of the *Briarwood*, and Captain P. W. Pennock of the *Temple Arch*, among others.

14. Dangerous Corner

FOR nine months during 1941 Tobruk was held as a fortress by the Eighth Army behind the enemy's lines. Its fame rivalled Malta's. During those months Tobruk was maintained and supplied from Alexandria, and the Merchant Navy had its part in the work. Merchant seamen were closely linked with every exploit in the Eastern Mediterranean ; they advanced and retreated with the Eighth Army ; they took our troops to Greece, withdrew with them to Crete, where a number were ashore with the soldiers ; and they took part in the evacuation to Egypt.

On May 10th, 1942, the Deputy Adjutant and Quartermaster-General of the Eighth Army visited the s.s. *Zealand* in Tobruk harbour, where she had just discharged a

FRONT LINE. In the Eastern Mediterranean the work of the merchant ships was woven into the operations of the Armies in Africa, Greece and Crete. Freighters travelled in the heart of the battle, their guns manned night and day.

cargo of petrol under bombing attacks, to tell the crew how much the Army appreciated their work. " You get more than your share of enemy bombs and torpedoes, but your job is to deliver the goods and splendidly you do it. The Army depends on you for a large proportion of its vital supplies. Eighth Army wants the ships' crews to know that it gives them a major share of the credit for the Army's successes."

The *Zealand* was almost a " Desert Rat " herself. So was the *Rodi*, now renamed the *Empire Patrol*. She survived two years of service in those waters. The Master of the *Zealand* (Captain Lancelot J. Branagan, O.B.E.) noted in January 1941 that occasional sandstorms left the ship covered with sand heavily charged with salt, and that night dews dissolved the salt into every crack and cranny and caused erosion to take place rapidly, while sand removed paint and varnish. Eye trouble caused by sand and flies was common and barked knuckles or abrasions took weeks to heal. Any desert soldier might have said the same. The ship was in Tobruk in December 1941 when a motor lighter full of cased benzine exploded alongside No. 2 hatch, setting the coamings and derrick guys of the *Zealand* alight. Captain Branagan adds : " The lighter had in the meantime brought up against a wreck under our stern which was used as a depth-charge store, and she kept the harbour well illuminated. Incidentally, this was my twenty-fifth wedding anniversary and the elegant celebrations were most appropriate".

The m.v. *Rodi* or *Empire Patrol* (Captain L. A. Williams) had a close acquaintance with Tobruk. She was in that harbour within a week of our first capturing the town in February 1941, and she was loaded for Tobruk when it fell in June 1942. She held one or two other enviable or unenviable records : she exploded two magnetic mines within 12 hours, and she was mined, in collision and on fire—all within 52 hours. The report of Mr. G. Victory, Chief Engineer, notes that among their other tasks they carried

British troops to Cyprus and Palestine and brought off Lieutenant-Colonel Keyes with his Commando after their attack behind the French lines in Syria—the same Lieutenant-Colonel Keyes who was later killed in an attack on Rommel's headquarters in Libya and posthumously awarded the V.C. Mr. Victory adds : " We could often leave the corvettes behind, especially if they were foul and overworked, and we treasured three signals received on different occasions, one of them—' H.M.S. —— regrets must request you to reduce speed'."

Greece and Crete offered as much excitement as did Tobruk. Captain R. P. Longstaff, D.S.C., of the *City of London*, describes his arrival in Kalamata Bay at 10.25 p.m. on April 26th, 1941, to assist in the evacuation. The night was black ; neither he nor two accompanying ships had the necessary charts, but they anchored close to land in fairly smooth water. Half an hour after midnight a destroyer came alongside packed with troops, who got aboard by gang planks, boatside ladders and so forth. This was done in complete darkness and almost dead silence. It was difficult to keep the troops moving, for they had had a hard time and many collapsed in sleep on the deck ; hot tea and cake were ready for them. By 4 a.m. 3,000 to 4,000 troops were aboard, mainly Australians, but also 400 British, besides Greeks and Yugoslavs. Half an hour later came the order to weigh and proceed. The next day was quiet. Aircraft flew over but did not attack. " During the afternoon", says Captain Longstaff, " the ubiquitous Scot appeared with a battered-looking set of bagpipes. He made persistent efforts to get music out of them, meeting with the disapproval of one Bren gunner, who cried out, ' Give me bloody dive-bombing any day'. However, the piper finally got his pipes going to the general amusement and entertainment."

No two ships had the same experience. Each one went through a small war of its own. Captain D. C. Lennie, O.B.E., of the m.v. *Santa Clara Valley*, after his ship was set on fire in an attack by 41 aircraft, fought that fire, which was burning next to a hold containing 200 tons of ammunition, throughout the night, and on reaching Nauplia had it under control. The ship had brought horses and mules, in addition to ammunition.

Captain J. D. Matthews, of the *Clan Cumming*, reports a night of dive-bombing in Pirus when a nearby ship was hit, and burned until she was red-hot fore and aft. He writes : " We concluded (wrongly) that if there were still high explosives on board they would have gone off before this, and I lay down half-dressed and was nearly asleep when the whole world seemed to burst asunder. The *Cumming* went over until she seemed to be on her beam ends and then rolled heavily for some time. All the woodwork in our rooms crashed down, and then came the rain of molten metal. Among other things we had a full plate 23 feet by 3 feet by $\frac{5}{8}$ of an inch wrapped round our main top, and about half her windlass had crashed through our No. 4 hatch and set fire to timber in our 'tween deck. . . . We got our fire hoses going and had the worst of our fires out when an officer of another ship hailed me, saying ' Our water system has failed, we are badly on fire with 50 tons of T.N.T. in No. 2 which will go up any time. Send a boat for us and abandon your own ship while you have time'. This was done in good order, a boat going to the other ship, and later that morning the captain and five of the crew returned and got the fires under".

But the Captain's adventures were not finished yet. His ship was sunk at sea by air attack eight days later and after five hours in the boats they were picked up by a Greek destroyer and landed at Megara, where the Greek Admiral, who had been in the destroyer, lent him a car and chauffeur to go to Athens. When the evacuation began Captain Matthews and his crew spent several nights in the open, living as best they could, obtaining food and an occasional lift from the military. He records : " Lived in a

cornfield for two days—luxury compared with the stony hillsides—and then had orders to embark at midnight for Crete. ' Every man to go as he stands and drop all baggage.' This was the unkindest cut, after we had all bought new clothes in Athens and at very high prices, too ". They reached Suda Bay and slept in fields which, he noted, were much softer than the Greek ones.

Our merchant seamen got thoroughly involved in the war in Crete. It was there that Cadet J. H. Dobson, B.E.M., of the s.s. *Dalesman*, when being marched in front of German parachutists, escaped, seizing a sub-machine-gun and turning it on his captors. He found his way to a New Zealand battery, which he assisted for some days. At length he arrived on the south side of the island and boarded a landing barge, where he found a mixed company of marines and troops. He undertook the navigation and after a passage of ten days reached Egypt. Two further facts are relevant : that this was Cadet Dobson's first voyage at sea, and that throughout his Crete exploits he was suffering from the effects of a rumbling appendix.

Chief Officer W. Rennie of the *Logician* (Captain W. Jones, O.B.E.) reports how parachute patrol parties were formed in Crete of gunners and seamen from his own ship and from the *Dalesman*, 24 men in each party under the command of a merchant officer. They slept on the ground or in slit trenches and arranged camouflage like soldiers.

The adventures quoted were only episodes among a wealth of solid work done by merchantmen in the Eastern Mediterranean. They and their crews are closely woven into the fabric of these campaigns. Whenever in the final victory a port was reopened, into it went the cargo ships : they had been ready, waiting, having been advised by the Army of probable dates of entry. Thus they moved on to Tobruk once more, to Benghazi and to Tripoli, until the Eastern Mediterranean was joined to the west.

15. "The Classic Convoy"

On the northern route to Russia, Britain's merchant seamen voyage dressed like Arctic explorers. On the Malta route, once they are in the Mediterranean, they usually wore tropical rig, officers in white ducks or shorts, gunners often stripped to the waist. If journeying to Murmansk and Archangel was the greater physical ordeal, Malta convoys over the brief period of 36 or 48 hours when they approached and passed Pantellaria endured from time to time the greater weight of attack. Nor was it always possible for the more powerful parts of the escorts—the battleships, aircraft carriers and heavy cruisers—to remain with the convoy throughout. Their departure on urgent missions or for other tactical reasons sometimes left the convoy in charge of lighter cruisers, destroyers, trawlers and motor launches. When that happened the Merchant Navy could feel a trifle naked, as a Master puts it ; and the ensuing E-boat attacks at night in the channel between Pantellaria and the Cape Bon peninsula—a stretch 50 or 60 miles in width—could take on a nightmarish quality.

Malta became an isolated outpost from the moment Italy entered the war in June 1940. Gibraltar lies 1,000 miles to the west and Alexandria not much nearer to the east. Drawn like a bow are Sicily—some 20 minutes distant in a bomber—Pantellaria, Tunisia and Libya. Steps had been taken to provision the island in the previous nine months of war, but it was obvious that some of the vital stocks would not last beyond the turn of the year. Only sea convoys could maintain her ; they were planned from both east and west (from Britain and from Egypt), and care was taken that each ship should be loaded with a diversity of cargo. This diversity in loading made secrecy unusually difficult.

Up to the end of 1941 the large majority of ships arrived safely. During the first nine months 24 ships were discharged in Malta, with 146,000 tons of cargo. A random example of what a typical ship carried in the shape of food supplies reads (in tons) : wheat 787, beans 723, rice 164, salt 12, coffee 49, eggs 83, soap 17, olive oil 12, onions 29, peanuts 30, oranges 13. But the necessities that were taken ranged from cement for building gun emplacements to forage for the goats on which the island's milk supply depends. There was a time when a shortage of babies' comforters raised a problem, but this was solved by air transport.

The m.v. *Port Chalmers* (Captain W. G. Higgs, O.B.E.), sailing in convoy from Britain in July 1941, took 2,000 tons of aviation spirit in 4-gallon tins. Other goods she carried were cement, maize, wheat, flour, whisky, tobacco, cigarettes, corned beef and mutton, bales of cloth, guns, shells, ammunition, cars, lorries and aircraft parts. Nor, although the convoys were attacked more heavily at a later stage, was her journey comfortable ; quite the reverse. Her escort included the battleship *Nelson*, the aircraft carrier *Ark Royal*, and the battle cruiser *Renown* from which Vice-Admiral Sir James Somerville sent a message to each Master saying : " Remember, everyone, that the watchword is THE CONVOY MUST GO THROUGH", prefacing this as follows : ". . . For over 12 months Malta has resisted all attacks of the enemy. The gallantry displayed by the garrison and people of Malta has aroused admiration throughout the world. To enable this defence to be continued it is essential that your ships, with their valuable cargoes, should arrive safely in the Grand Harbour.

" Don't make smoke. Don't show any lights at night—a torch can be seen for miles. If you have to signal by day or night, use the lowest possible power light. Keep good station and don't straggle. If your ship is damaged, keep her going at the best possible speed.

" Provided every officer and man realises that it is up to him to do his duty to the very

BOUND FOR MALTA. The little convoy moves towards the enemy. It will most certainly be attacked. As the first inevitable bomber approaches from starboard the lookout on the escorting cruiser gives the alarm.

best of his ability, then I feel sure we shall succeed, because we of the Royal Navy have the greatest confidence in you, our brother seamen of the Merchant Navy."

Before the convoy reached Gibraltar the *Nelson* exercised them in emergency turns for two hours, afterwards raising a smile everywhere by the human signal, "Time for supper". The ships also did some practice shooting.

They passed Gibraltar but saw nothing of it ; dense fog enveloped the whole convoy for over an hour. It was a very anxious time for the nine big ships in close formation ; one could not see either the ship ahead or the one on either side. The *Port Chalmers* switched on her navigation lights at full power and the *Deucalion*, which was ahead, hung a large cargo cluster over her stern. At daybreak

the cruiser *Edinburgh* flashed to the *Port Chalmers* : " You were a long way astern even before fog came down. It is vital that close station be kept both day and night". Captain Higgs writes : " We accepted the reproof meekly". A day or two later came another message, this time from the cruiser *Manchester*, saying : " S stands for Straggler and Sunk". The merchantman was then two cables astern of station and coming up fast.

That was at 9.15 a.m. Nineteen minutes later nine hostile aircraft came in sight flying in three arrowheads, and *Nelson* made the signal to " stagger". Shortly afterwards both escort and convoy opened fire. The air, writes Captain Higgs, vibrated with thunderous crashes. Bombs were dropping among the ships but none was hit. The naval liaison officer on the *Fort Chalmers's* bridge was shouting : " Hit the ——, hit one of them, for God's sake ! "

More attacks were made during the day but none was dive-bombing. The aircraft were all judged to be Italian ; there was no lack of courage on the part of the low-flying torpedo bombers. At 5.30 p.m., *Renown*, *Nelson* and the *Ark Royal* left at high speed for the north west, taking some destroyers with them, but the cruiser *Edinburgh* and several destroyers remained.

In the early hours of next day an attack by E-boats was made. " We couldn't see them— we ourselves had no searchlights," said one master. " You had to shout to hear yourself speak. The warships began to sweep round with their own searchlights, and red tracer began to fly. There must have been 20 of these E-boats. Suddenly the cruiser *Edinburgh's* searchlight steadied—these searchlights now lit up the scene—and we saw a small object on the surface. The cruiser let go what must have been a complete broadside. Spray leapt up from a score of places and when it subsided the small object had gone. Cruisers and destroyers were now using searchlights and guns all round the convoy. The *Durham* turned away to port to avoid running into the tracer ahead of her, and after a moment's hesitation I followed her, thinking she had seen something invisible to me. We both resumed convoy course and increased to full speed, taking care to remain within the destroyer screen. At 4 a.m. the attack ceased, but about that time I felt two rumbling explosions that shook the ship. For a moment I thought we were hit by torpedo, but I was wrong. At 5 a.m. we were all formed up again. Later I learned that *Durham* claimed to have rammed an E-boat during the action."

During the hot 36 hours men had lived on sandwiches and jugs of coffee ; they had slept little and slept fully clothed. The welcome in Malta harbour rejoiced them, for this harbour, built as though fashioned for greeting, had its bastions black with

people cheering, and General Dobbie came aboard to shake hands.

The merchantmen lay with two anchors ahead and tied to the wharf astern and unloaded into lighters, a task of 15 working days. Air raids numbered five a week, but most of the crews continued to live on board. They had the pleasure of hearing the Italian communiqué claiming to have sunk 70,000

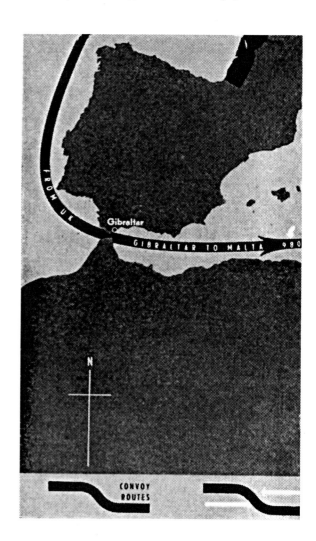

tons of our ships : in fact the convoy totalled only 58,114 tons and all arrived.

During the months from February to August 1942 the Malta convoys became steadily more perilous. Eighty-five merchant-men sailed, of which 24 were sunk and 11 had to return to port. Of ships sailing from Britain, 15 out of 40 were lost. From Egypt during this time 296,000 tons of cargo were shipped and 34 per cent. of it lost ; from Britain 314,690 tons were shipped and 43 per cent. lost. These figures tell something of the achievement and of the price that was paid. At this time only one or two tankers could be sent—the famous *Ohio* (Captain D. W. Mason, G.C.) was one—and the bulk of aviation spirit and petrol was shipped in cases and drums and, on arrival in Malta,

THE MALTA LIFELINE.

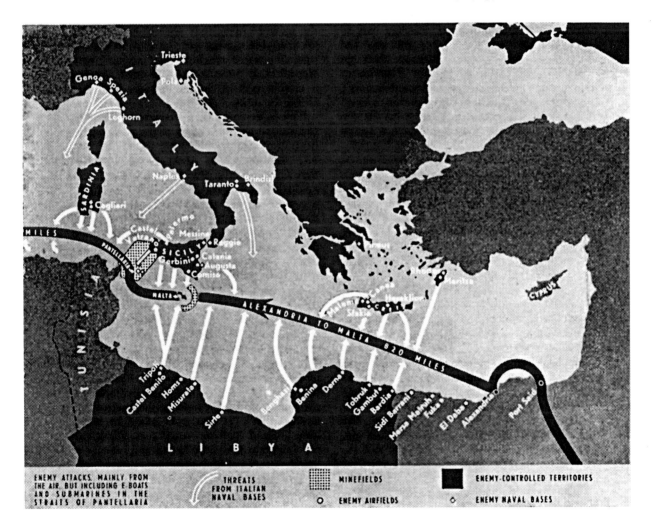

ENEMY ATTACKS MAINLY FROM THE AIR, BUT INCLUDING E-BOATS AND SUBMARINES IN THE STRAITS OF PANTELLARIA — THREATS FROM ITALIAN NAVAL BASES — MINEFIELDS — ENEMY CONTROLLED TERRITORIES — ENEMY AIRFIELDS — ENEMY NAVAL BASES

distributed over the island to make it as invulnerable as possible.

A convoy of six merchant ships sailed from the Clyde in June 1942, escorted by two heavy cruisers and a number of destroyers and sloops. At Gibraltar a battleship and two aircraft carriers joined them.

The ships had been at sea for ten days before the first air attacks were made. "The heaviest", writes Captain Nelson Rice, of the m.v. *Orari*, " came in the early evening south of Sardinia." The number of aircraft was not short of 50, but " our fighters put up such a good show and the ships' barrage was so intense that very few planes got near the merchant ships". He estimates that 30 enemy were shot down, our Hurricanes from the aircraft carriers being outstanding in fire work. The account of another officer, Mr. Ross Vincent, says that earlier in the day, in a torpedo bombing attack, a heavy cruiser was hit and a Dutch merchantman set on fire so that she sank in five minutes. During that night, as they sailed through the straits between Panteliaria and the mainland, flares were seen at intervals but no attack occurred. " At dawn, on the northern horizon," he continues, " loomed a fleet which we thought was probably our own returning from a scouting expedition during the night. . . . But we were not long left in doubt as the whine of shells soon filled the air, and then they straddled us."

"The warships", writes Captain Rice, " proved to be two 8-inch Italian cruisers and five destroyers, but although their shelling was fairly accurate at such long range, not a ship was hit and we soon had the protection of a smoke-screen laid by our escort. Although heavily outgunned, our escort was magnificent ; *Cairo* and the destroyers dashed between us and laid the smoke-screen, turning west as they did so. We turned west into the screen, heading back for Tunisian territorial waters, while *Cairo* and the destroyers sailed into the attack and succeeded in heading the enemy up north ; nice work, when one considers

that 4.7 guns were the heaviest our ships could muster.

" Soon, out of the blue, came the first Axis dive-bombers from Sicily and the day's fun was on. The *Chant*, on our starboard beam, was soon hit, listed badly and became well ablaze. She caused us some uncomfortable moments by careering over towards us ; knowing what she was loaded with, we stood not upon the order of our going, and thanked the powers for that extra touch of speed the *Orari* can produce in a tight corner.

" The *Chant's* crew didn't stay to discuss the matter either, they got out and over by all available means, but she sank so rapidly that the water reached her ' ammo ' first. Her oil tanks burst as she went down, leaving a terrific pall of fire and smoke that was visible for most of the day."

The fight continued throughout the day, *Orari's* gun-crews stripped to the waist in the heat, and cheering whenever an aircraft was hit. Another great cheer went up when they sighted Malta about 4 p.m.—just a blur on the horizon on the port bow. " The enemy appeared to put everything into an attack shortly afterwards ; the Spitfires were decoyed away by low-flying planes and then from the skies in all directions came the Ju.s. *Troilus* (Captain W. G. Harrison, C.B.E.), *Cairo* and ourselves all disappeared from each other's view in columns of water and spray from near misses ; they did everything but hit us." As they neared the harbour the enemy were dropping mines. Two destroyers and a minesweeper were mined and the *Orari* herself struck one half a mile off the harbour, in water through which *Troilus* had just passed. Luckily, the mine exploded in the only hold which held neither petrol nor ammunition ! It was past midnight when they entered harbour—only two left of the six merchantmen that began this voyage— but the people of Malta had not gone to bed ; they were on the bastions cheering. The crew had a cup of tea, " topped derricks ", and before daylight the cargo was being unloaded. That morning Lord Gort

THE GATEWAY TO THE FORTRESS. A narrow channel of water between Sicily and North Africa, bridged by Luftwaffe and heavily mined, became to every relieving convoy a gateway of fire to Malta. This convoy of August is running that stretch of sea. The blue skies scorch black with shells bursting in the path of the raiders. A mor later a bomb explodes between the two ships seen above while the escort's swinging pom-pom follows the Stuka's (

THE OHIO COMES THROUGH. She was torpedoed, lamed, and set on fire in the August convoy. The tail of a dive-bomber fell on her decks. Her boilers blew up and her engines failed. Taken in tow by two escort ships she reached Malta, two days late, but with her cargo safe.

visited the ship to congratulate them.

Not all ships sailing to Malta voyaged in convoy. A number in 1941 sailed alone, the Admiralty, shipping companies, and Masters exercising a combined ingenuity as to how it could best be done and the enemy hoodwinked. Losses were heavy, but the vessels which got through were vital in keeping the fortress in being. One ship which reached Malta thus was sunk on the homeward voyage, and the crew interned in North Africa for 15 months until the Allied expedition arrived.

Another merchantman, the m.v. *Pampas* (Captain E. B. Ingram, O.B.E.), made a remarkable voyage in which she started from Alexandria in March 1942 in company with three other cargo vessels, but after fights with enemy aircraft in stormy weather, in

which the gun crews were constantly drenched in heavy spray and the armament streaming with water (for the Mediterranean can be a very rough sea), she voyaged alone. During the air attacks she had already struck a torpedo bomber direct on the nose and shattered it.

Every convoy to Malta had incidents which were its own. For example, Captain W. H. Matheson, of the *City of Calcutta*, speaking of January 1942, tells how, as three merchant ships were in single line ahead with destroyers on either side, all of them fighting off over 50 Ju. 88s, the cruiser *Penelope* sailed up and down the line broadcasting encouraging remarks to them. When he and his vessel sailed again for Malta five months later from Port Said, a bomb explosion lifted the ship almost bodily out of the water, putting main engines and lighting out of action, and he was ordered to try to reach Tobruk—as stormy a port of refuge as ever a ship had. Yet in Tobruk she was repaired ; divers plugged as many of the rivet holes as possible (1,000 had been sheered and two laps of shell plating opened, one for 18 feet and the other for 22 feet), and finally she left with 500 troops hard-lying on her deck at a time when the battle raging at Knightsbridge was clearly discernible. Tobruk fell to the enemy a week later.

No convoy had a stiffer battle than that which sailed from Britain in August 1942, and brought some relief to the fortress. The *Port Chalmers* (Captain H. G. B. Pinkney, D.S.O.), the *Deucalion* (Captain P. J. Pycraft, O.B.E.), and the m.v. *Melbourne Star* (Captain D. R. Macfarlane, D.S.O., O.B.E.), had run the hazards before, in July 1941. His Majesty's ships *Nelson*, *Cairo* and *Manchester*, which were part of the escort in the Mediterranean, were old friends of these convoys, too. The *Melbourne Star* was loaded with 1,350 tons of high octane petrol, 700 tons of kerosene, 1,450 tons of high explosive and several thousand tons of heavy oil ; it is moments in the voyage, as seen by Captain Macfarlane, that are mainly described here.

Enemy reconnaissance aircraft had shadowed the convoy for several days before they entered the Mediterranean, but nothing of note, he remarks, happened until two days past Gibraltar when, a few minutes after 1 p.m. on August 11th, three or four explosions were felt, and looking westward, he saw the aircraft carrier *Eagle* heeling over and her own planes slipping off her decks into the sea. A pilot bravely tried to take his aircraft off the sloping deck but it was heeling so fast that he could not do it.

Later in the afternoon the first air attacks began, and went on till after dark. Quiet fell until daylight next morning, when bombing attacks were renewed and continued throughout the day. About noon the merchantman *Deucalion* was hit by bombs and left behind with a destroyer guarding

her, but unhappily the *Deucalion* was sunk later that day.

The air attack grew in intensity about 7 p.m., just before the battleships and carriers were due to leave, and it was then that the carrier *Indomitable* was hit. " It was a most impressive sight to see her anti-aircraft guns firing away through the flames as she steamed towards the setting sun." The *Indomitable's* aircraft had done very fine work. On that day fully 260 enemy planes had attacked, and of 39 shot down the *Indomitable's* aircraft had accounted for a large proportion. Two hours later the convoy was changing formation when U-boats added their attack to that of dive-torpedo and high-level bombers. In the ensuing battle two warships were hit, the tanker *Ohio* was torpedoed but far from sunk, a merchant vessel was hit and blew up, and another was bombed and set on fire so that she had later to be abandoned ; the *Brisbane Star* (Captain F. M. Riley, D.S.O.) was hit also.

Turn now for a moment to the tanker *Ohio* which ultimately reached Malta two days after the *Melbourne Star*. The chief officer, Mr. Douglas H. Gray, had just finished his watch and was still on the bridge. " When the torpedo struck," he says, " the ship shook violently, steering gear broke, and all communication with the engine-room and after-end of the ship was cut off, with the exception of the telephone, which was still working. Fire broke out in the pump-room. We made an attempt to get the compressor started forward. The engineers were all down below. . . ." About an hour later the vessel was under way and Mr. Gray remained on the poop deck throughout the night carrying out the Captain's orders and steering the ship from that position. At 6 a.m. next day they rejoined the convoy. The respite was brief. Two hours later their guns were in action again. During that morning a Stuka which had dropped several near misses had its tail shot off ; the tail landed on the *Ohio's* poop. " In the same forenoon", says Mr. Gray, " the second boiler blew out and the

WITHIN THE FORTRESS. With clusters of lights hung in their rigging, the ships that mean life to Malta unload their cargoes through the night.

engines stopped. I was still steering from aft and the Captain gave me instructions to come forward and make fast the tow to a destroyer which had offered to assist us. After I had made fast the tow, I came aft and disconnected the steam steering gear and connected up chain blocks to move the rudder, as the destroyer hadn't enough weigh to tow us and the *Ohio* was going round in circles. . . . We proceeded in this manner for about an hour, when the tow rope parted". A destroyer took them off but put them aboard again at 6 p.m. and they were towed by the destroyer *Penn* and the minesweeper *Rye*. They were again steering with chain blocks and had let go the paravane gear. Half an hour later another air raid occurred ; the *Ohio* was hit in the engine-room, and the boiler-room was wrecked.

Orders were given to abandon ship, and Mr. Gray along with others was picked up by a motor launch. Darkness was falling and a heavy raid was still centred upon the ship.

The *Melbourne Star* had continued to be in the thick of it. She had had to put her helm hard a-port and increase speed to avoid a collision just after the heavy fight in which the *Ohio* was first disabled, and she later found herself proceeding towards Malta, with two other ships following but, for the moment, unable to see any escort. However, as she neared Cape Bon lighthouse, a destroyer overtook her. They followed the destroyer inside the minefields but eventually lost her on account of her speed while, on the other hand, the *Melbourne Star* outdistanced the two ships following behind. She observed great activity ahead in the shape of tracer shells and bullets, which suggested E-boat attacks, but fortunately when she reached that spot all was quiet again. Captain Macfarlane adds : " We were giving a wonderful fireworks display from our exhaust and I was very perturbed about it. Everything possible had been done to stop it, without success". Soon afterwards two things happened—they came up to a destroyer escort, and they received an S O S by wireless that a merchantman was torpedoed and stopped. The *Melbourne Star* zigzagged to the south of the destroyers, trying at intervals to drop in astern of one of them ; during this period she observed a very heavy explosion to the northward. Some time later she was able to rejoin the main body of the convoy coming up astern, and took up her station behind the *Waiwarama* (Captain R. S. Pearce).

" At 8.10 a.m.", reports Captain Macfarlane, " dive-bombers suddenly came out of the sun and a stick of bombs fell on the *Waiwarama*, which blew up and disappeared in a few seconds. We were showered with debris from this ship. A piece of plating five feet long fell on board. The base of a steel ventilator, half an inch thick and two feet six inches high, partly demolished one of our machine-gun posts. At the same time a piece of angle iron narrowly missed a cadet. The sea was one sheet of fire and as we were so close we had to steam through it. I put the helm hard a-port and had to come down from where I was on monkey island to the bridge to save myself from being burned. It seemed as though we had been enveloped in flame and smoke for years, although it was only a matter of minutes, otherwise the ship could never have survived. The flames were leaping mast high—indeed, air pilots reported that at times they reached 2,000 feet. The heat was terrific. The air was becoming drier every minute, as though the oxygen was being sucked out of it, as, in fact, it was. When we inspected the damage afterwards, we found that nearly all the paint on the ship's sides had been burnt away, and the bottoms of the lifeboats reduced to charcoal."

Unable to see how they could avoid being blown up as they sailed through the flames, Captain Macfarlane had ordered everybody forward ; however, they cleared the fire safely and he thereupon ordered everybody back to stations. It was now reported to him that 36 men were missing. " These men, thinking that the for'ard end of the ship had been struck and being quite certain that if they stayed aboard they would be blown up, jumped over the side. All our defences had now to be reorganised. Throughout the action my men behaved splendidly ; the team spirit was perfect, but after the loss of their comrades they were more keen than ever and we could not hold them back." (Twenty-two of the 36 men were picked up by a destroyer and the *Ohio*.)

Further air attacks occurred in which a merchantman was lost and the *Ohio* again damaged, but from the time the escort from Malta met them the voyage was without further excitement. They reached Malta in company with two other merchantmen ; a fourth arrived on the next day, and the *Ohio* in tow the day after. The *Melbourne Star* had been in Malta over 12 hours before it was discovered that a 6-inch shell had landed during the voyage on top of the Master's day-room, smashing deck planking and setting in but not penetrating the steel deck—all this without exploding.

In all, 40 convoys sailed to Malta, eight of them from Britain. Their success kept the fortress in being and enabled it to play its vital part both in disrupting Rommel's supply lines and finally assisting our armies to free Africa. Malta's supplies, both food and ammunition, became perilously low more than once. The people's ration fell to 10½ ounces of bread a day plus a little coffee mixed with barley, a few ounces of rice and a meagre sugar allowance. The Government's communal meal was vegetable soup, a few beans and a slice of corned beef or a little tinned fish.

Without the merchantmen's timely arrival, the fortress must have fallen.

16.   Armadas to North Africa

VICTORY in war depends on half a dozen factors, but without good supplies and good transport it is impossible. At the start of an expedition each soldier needs 10 tons of material, and after that half a ton a month to keep him going. In the Western Desert the British forces twice reached Benghazi and twice had to fall back because they outran men and material—they were too thin on the ground. Rommel suffered likewise ; at El Alamein he was stretched to the uttermost. The Axis were finally overthrown in Africa and suffered disaster chiefly because their armies were to all intents and purposes cut off from their sources of supply ; whereas the British commissariat worked with immense efficiency, and the pincer movements executed by merchantmen and wheeled transport kept pace with the thrusts and advances of the Eighth and First Armies.

General Alexander, in a message to Lord Leathers expressing the gratitude of the Army to the Allied Merchant Navies, said : " The success of the Merchant Navies' undertaking is proved by the weight of men and metal brought across the oceans of the world, thus enabling our Forces to defeat the Axis in Egypt and Libya and prepare for further efforts elsewhere. We honour them for their courage and steadfastness in the face of assaults of the enemy and the perils of the seas ".

This movement of supplies for the final North African campaign, journeying on the one hand 12,000 miles via the Cape to Suez, and on the other direct to Tunisia by way of the Straits of Gibraltar, handled about 4,000,000 tons of cargo, a total divided fairly equally between the two routes. The periods covered were, however, different : the building-up and strengthening of the Middle East in readiness for the break through at

ALGIERS, 1942. The offensive is on. Part of the merchant fleet that brought an army to the new battle front crowds the great harbour and its approaches. A smoke screen protects it against enemy attack.

El Alamein is (for our purpose here) judged to have begun about March 1942, seven months before the North African expedition sailed. In each case the period ends in March 1943. During those 12 months there were transported to the Middle East via the Cape 70,000 vehicles including guns, 2,000 tanks, 600 aircraft and 150 locomotives. In addition some 2,200 fighter and bomber aircraft were shipped to Takoradi, on the west coast of Africa, to be flown thence to the Middle East. The quantities recorded do not include supplies of the highest importance brought from the United States in American ships, among them the fast ships carrying the Sherman tanks so promptly sent to our assistance by President Roosevelt after the fall of Tobruk.

Maintenance of the Middle East as a strong base called for vision and from time to time great courage. It is no secret now that Mr. Churchill dispatched troops and vital supplies to General Wavell's desert army when those men on the high seas might, if history had written itself otherwise, have been sorely needed in Britain to resist invasion. Another dilemma had to be faced early in 1942. No one could foresee, when new divisions left British shores in April, May and June, whether they (or some of them) would be needed to resist a Japanese attack on India, a fresh thrust at Egypt, or to support Russia by moving through Iraq. The decision was not finally taken till the first ships approached Aden ; Egypt was the choice, and the Eighth Army was so strengthened that Rommel was overthrown. Long-range planning had yielded its reward.

From the outbreak of war up to July 1942 the Merchant Navy had carried to the Middle East nearly a million men. Up to February 1943, troopships had transported some 3,000,000 men all over the world, with a loss of only 1,348 killed or drowned.

Britain's lines of communication round the Cape to Port Tewfik or Alexandria were the longest history has ever known. Sailing to New Zealand would have been as easy a task. The time occupied was usually 80 days, or two and two-thirds months. The discharging of one cargo and loading of another in the Middle East took another 30 days; if a cargo ship were then required to call at India or elsewhere and reload, it would not be likely to do more than one and a half round voyages in the year. If cargo were not available in the Middle East or India, the vessel often returned to Britain via South America either in ballast or carrying coal from South Africa to South America; thence it might go with bauxite to North America, reloading there for the United Kingdom. Refrigerated ships, after a voyage to Suez, frequently journeyed to Australasia or the River Plate and loaded there for home.

Voyages to the Middle East have been as varied in hazard as the sea itself varies in mood. The neighbourhood of Freetown has, at times, been no less dangerous than the North Atlantic; open-boat journeys in those tropic seas have entailed sufferings from sun and thirst as dire as the sufferings caused by bitter winds and tumultuous seas. But, again, the fast convoys—and especially troop convoys—have often enjoyed voyages that were more like pleasure cruises. Lads in the Army, who had seldom looked at the sea, and ships' boys and stewards afloat for the first time, have on this voyage watched shoals of flying fish scudding across the green-blue sea like swallows, and round about the Cape of Good Hope they have seen whales blowing. Soldiers and airmen have hung over the rail and observed that even at midnight the water can be lilac in colour and the sky dotted with white, fleecy clouds, and found to their surprise that, close to the Equator there may be days of wind and grey sea, such as are common off the English coast. On dark evenings they have seen a dark sea lit with phosphorescent stars, as though a piece of sky had dropped into the water, and the convoy has appeared to move in a patch of ghostly light. Altogether, the journey to the Middle East, were it reasonably free from alarms, could be a refreshment and delight, until South Africa was left well behind and the torrid heat of the Red Sea bore down on the ship.

No such armadas of ships as those which sailed to North Africa in October and November 1942 have ever stirred the face of the waters. At one moment over 200 ships were on the seas from Britain and 70 from the United States. In the ensuing six months over 1,000 left the United Kingdom, among them liners whose names are household words, besides tankers, tramp ships, colliers, and coasters. In addition to the First Army and its reinforcements, those ships took to Africa 394 aircraft, 63,784 vehicles, 901 tanks, 3,677 guns and six locomotives and tenders. Cased petrol amounted to 239,796 tons, bulk oil 67,188 tons, coal 345,713 tons, and other stores 769,321 tons. But this was not all that was done. To Gibraltar were sent hundreds of thousands of tons of stores and equipment months earlier, and to Gibraltar also were shipped 1,416 aircraft, which flew onwards to various landing grounds farther east.

The British store transports which carried equipment for the first assault parties were loaded for Oran, Algiers and Bougie; within three weeks others were dispatched to Philippeville and Bone. As troops moved east, the merchantmen kept pace with them; coasters and colliers moved to and fro along the African coast from first to last.

A few of the incidental items transported during the campaign throw light on what modern war means: thus, there were sent 450,000,000 cigarettes, 9,000,000 bars of chocolate, 500,000 lb. of soap, 7,000 tons of barbed wire ; while to and from the United Kingdom went 71,000 bags of mail.

Organisation of the North African convoys required months of hard work ; joint meetings of War Transport, War Office, Navy and United States Headquarters staffs took place twice a day ; to work 16 hours a day was commonplace.

Ships' crews and dockers were equally full of zest. When a vessel ran into foul weather on the way to the port of loading, and damage was done to boats and super-structure, it was the crew who, sensing some-thing remarkable afoot, did the repairs. A Sea Transport Officer turned 60 did not sleep ashore for eight days. Ninety of those officers sailed with the convoys.

Finding and choosing the right ships for the right ports and landing beaches were intensely difficult. Military commanders had, first of all, to decide precisely what they wanted, and where. After that was known came the task of selecting the ships and loading the correct materials to the correct plan. Loading was tactical : tanks, guns and stores had to come out of the ship in the right order, weapons ready to fight. A lot of vehicles sailed with steel slings under their wheels, prepared for lifting. Risks were taken : vehicles were aboard with petrol inside them.

Decks were heavily loaded with landing craft, yet when the convoys, after battling with heavy weather in the Atlantic, passed Gibraltar, cargoes were intact : nothing had shifted. That was because loading had been expert. To that end, ship plans, akin to those of an architect, are kept by War Transport for every ship. Models the size of dominoes are used to represent vehicles ; former ships' captains work with rulers and set-squares, for inches in the height of 'tween decks or coamings are important in the planning of stowage.

Convoys to North Africa have proved far less perilous than those individual ones to Russia or Malta, on which the fiercest attacks happened to be made, but they have had to fight none the less. Merchantmen have given and taken hard blows. After a heavy bomb-ing attack in a North African port a Master could count 250 holes of one sort or another in his ship ; another expended 16,000 rounds in her six months' journeying.

Bone was the most forward port and British ships using it endured attacks from the beginning of the campaign. The *Orient City*, for example (Captain W. V. Doughty), was in Bone for 12 days from November 13th, 1942, onwards. During that period she was bombed regularly both day and night, and used in reply 9,000 rounds of Oerlikon ammunition and 140 rounds of 12-pounder. She took to Bone 195 vehicles, each with five tons of ammunition in it, and a mixed cargo which included 900 tons of high octane spirit. The ship was not hit, except that a funnel stay was struck by a splinter, but there was a night when few of the crew expected to see the dawn. Soldier pioneers during one day unloaded 85 vehicles and 500 tons of ammunition under constant bombing and machine-gunning, the captain of pioneers descending the hold to work with his hands alongside his men.

Ships in Algiers and Bougie were often under attack also. But these air attacks, coupled with those of U-boats, inflicted only slight shipping losses, no more than some 2 per cent.

It is to the Middle East and North Africa that most of the voyages of our troopships have so far been made. Troopships have also served India, the Far East, Australia, Madagascar, New Zealand, Norway ; and an increasing host of soldiers and airmen has been brought from the U.S.A. and Canada. But it is to Africa that the principal troop convoys have sailed. The work has

TROOPSHIP. She may well have been here before, with peacetime passengers and freight. Now her passengers are fighting-men, her paint is battledress, her decks jut with turrets of concrete. Across the moving bridge of ships like her the Allied armies poured into Africa.

been done in the main by passenger liners, vessels familiar to thousands of happy folk in times of peace.

The ships have a soberer look to-day. Painted dark grey, their names almost obliterated, their upper structures given a curious weighty and solid look by the addition of steel plates and plastic wall—a mixture of cork, bitumastic and cement—and by armament ensconced in circular steel-walled pits, the ships are a vital part of the war machine. Had Britain not possessed these fleets of liners, Africa could not have been freed nor America's hosts been brought so readily to these shores. No other nation could have done the transportation; none other had the ships. To enable them to carry their troops in requisite number, the interiors of the ships have been largely transformed. Swimming baths have usually been bridged and turned into dormitories; cabins which held one or two people house four or six; dining-rooms feed 1,000 or even 2,000 men at a time. Decks on which nothing more serious than quoits was played now echo to commands of physical training instructors keeping men fit and alert. The ship's complement of men to man her guns may easily number 250, working in three watches. An eye has to be kept on troops to see they do not use the automatic lamps, fitted in rafts and ships' boats, for reading at night.

It needs little imagination to realise the heavy responsibility falling on the Master and crew of such a vessel. A Master who sailed to Algiers and back in April 1943 said he never took his clothes off except in Algiers. He slept 1½ hours during the day and an hour or so at night, if he were lucky. U-boat alarms numbered two a day; Focke-Wulfs circled round but did not attack. The ship avoided one or two floating mines only by quick manœuvring.

In spite (or because) of the thousands of officers and men under his charge, the Captain's is a lonely life. In dangerous waters he sleeps in his chair, never unaware of the tramping of the officer on watch, so many paces this way, so many that. If the footsteps cease or the pace varies, he is instantly awake. This ceaseless, tireless vigil is one reason, at all events, why the loss of life on troopships has been extremely small. It was a Master of vast experience who said that a troopship is really a naval ship flying the Red Ensign instead of the White.

---

17. The Sicily Landings

THE general outline of the plan for the invasion of Sicily in July 1943 was discussed at the Casablanca Conference in January—so far ahead are plans made.

To Casablanca went planning men from the Ministry of War Transport, and others journeyed later to Algiers to keep in touch with General Eisenhower's Headquarters Staff; still others went to the Middle East. In both centres preparations were carried out in minute detail, even to the use of models of tanks and vehicles for planning the tactical stowage and loading. Much had been learnt in the North African campaign.

The sailings to Sicily were three-pronged—from the United Kingdom, from North Africa, and from the Middle East. So that the assault ships from Middle East might be available at the right time, they left Britain months before, taking troops to Suez but carrying landing craft instead of lifeboats at the ships' davits. Exercises and rehearsals were carried out en route.

Not only men but the ships also had to be prepared. The cargo ships for the assault convoys and the convoys immediately following included among them Norwegian, Dutch, American, Polish and Belgian ships, as well as British. They had to be capable of lifting L.C.M.s (landing craft mechanised) with their own gear, and in a number of vessels derricks had to be " boosted " in order to do it. The carriage of petrol required the sheathing of a hold with timber, the fitting of gas extractors, and the provision of special fire-fighting equipment. It was necessary that ships should be in a condition to undertake an ocean voyage immediately after unloading : with this end in view tons of ballast were placed in the lower holds of most ships. Where the ammunition and stores were not enough to form a platform on which vehicles could be loaded, a floor had to be made of ballast surfaced with timber. In two convoys sailing from the Middle East 10,000 lorry loads of sand were used as ballast for this purpose.

When the time came, vessels were loaded at ports in the Bristol Channel and the north-west coast of Britain, at Alexandria, Beirut and Haifa, and others in Algiers which had previously sailed from the United Kingdom with mechanical transport, L.C.M.s and stores. The assault convoy starting from Britain rehearsed a full-scale exercise before it left on its appointed task.

When making the North African landings, the Allies had expected only slight opposition ; and so far as the British landings went that expectation was fulfilled. In Sicily we prepared for fierce opposition, and these preparations made the Merchant Navy's task more difficult. Throughout the voyages to Sicily, when some ships were lost, and during the assault landings, precautions were never relaxed ; everything was done in the expectation, from moment to moment, that strenuous fighting would develop. Weather, which had been perfect for a long period but broke up within 24 hours of the assault, brought its own anxieties.

Captain David W. Bone, C.B.E., Master of one of the ships taking part, writes : " We made an exact rendezvous with the slower ships of our convoy. . . . As the afternoon drew on, the marvellous precision of the whole great operation was made clear to us. Within

sight to the eastward were the convoys from the Levant, and on our port hand the huge floats of the United States forces". Among them were L.S.T.s (landing ships tank) and L.C.I.s (landing craft infantry), which had crossed the Atlantic under their own power, making history by doing so.

" The wind", says Captain Bone, " had been quickly increasing from about noon and now stood at about moderate gale force with a heavy beam sea running. This aroused some disquiet ; indeed, there were opinions that the whole operation might be ' stymied ' on account of the weather. . . . I held the opinion that the wind would lessen after sunset—and this was, later, borne out. . . .

" We did not see the Sicilian mainland before darkness set in. Ahead of us in our formation there were only the flagship of our force and the naval vessels of the escort, which now included fleet minesweepers towing a path for the force. Our particular convoy was in two columns and ranged astern almost as far as one could see ; elsewhere the horizon was blanked out by smaller vessels hurrying from the Maltese harbours . . . they lurched and drove almost bows under in maintaining the speed of the convoy.

" We had the moon at first quarter, and even after moonset at about 11 p.m. the weather was so clear that we had no difficulty in maintaining station, although a very keen look-out had to be kept for the frequent and sudden appearance of the smaller craft close-to. Of course, no lights were shown and even dim blue signalling was not often resorted to. . . . My recollection is of a very great silence in the ship, broken only from time to time by a stout Canadian voice at the microphone telling the troops off to their stations in the landing craft.

" Moon set at about 11 . . . From early daybreak we had been in expectation of attack from the air. . . . Now, with daylight gone, we had reasonable assurance that only moored mines and action from the coastal batteries were to be expected. But our gallant minesweepers were spurring steadily ahead and the dim blue lights on their Oropesa floats took no sudden dive, nor did the flash of gunfire lighten up the sea line ahead. I think everyone on the navigation bridge was puzzled at this. I know I was. . . . That we would be spotted by this time was almost a foregone conclusion, and even the sleepiest and most muddleheaded of enemy observers could not, we thought, miss so vast a fleet. . . . At about midnight, however, we made out the rays of searchlights ahead. All were directed upward to the sky."

At this beach no single searchlight was directed seaward ; no gunfire from the shore batteries. The aircraft bombing Paccino took all their attention. The ships' speed was reduced at midnight and preparations

were made to anchor in 38 fathoms. As they did so, tremors occurred in the ships from the bursting of bombs ashore. It was now quite dark, albeit clear, and only the bulk of the nearest ships could be made out. The signals from the flagship were brief : " Stop engines and take way off ship", and then, "Anchor". Not an easy matter within the narrow ribbon of a swept channel with ships of many types, each with her own way of idling when steerage way was lost ; but it was well and safely done and in very complete silence, anchors being paid out in gear. Now the whine of winches was heard and quiet but decisive orders on the loud hailers : " Craft numbers so and so. Stand by " ; and then " Lower away ". The wind had fallen light, but a heavy swell was running.

TUNISIA HAS FALLEN, AND A NEW INVASION FLEET GATHERS OFF THE COAST OF AFRICA.   THIS IS PART

A second release of landing craft occurred ; and later on, while the greater body of troops was still on board, work was done in sorting out troops' equipment, which ranged from traffic signs to tablets for purifying drinking water. Later the larger troop-carrying craft came alongside. The swell remained considerable ; men had to use the scramble-nets and long-side ladders and trust to a timely leap as the craft below surged up and down.

Soon the " Success " signal came through —the beaches had been secured—and the speed of disembarkation was now accelerated. When daylight grew, an hour later, the whole of the ships lay as planned, many within a stone's throw of the places marked out for them on charts months before. Escorting destroyers now threw a smokescreen round

the ships and within this screen they weighed anchor and moved to the inshore anchorages —a proceeding in which they had frequently to anchor and weigh again, sighting little more than the masts of their leader above the smokescreen. Meanwhile, heavy naval guns were shelling the island on a nor'-west bearing. " The smack of salvos sounded perilously close," says Captain Bone, " and it was physically impossible to restrain a nervous reaction at each succeeding impact on the ears—although we all wore gunfire plugs. Light airs occasionally came from the land and in them there was a faint scent of orange or lemon groves, but this was quickly overthrown by the acrid whiff of cordite fumes as we passed through a heavy patch or two. . . . The broad of day found us

WAITING, HALF A MILLION TONS OF SHIPPING AIMED FOR SICILY, THE SOUTHERN GATE TO EUROPE

SHIPS ON THE MARCH. The invasion fleet, bearing the first wave of assault troops, moves towards Sicily. Darkness draws on. Arrival at the south coast of the island is timed for midnight.

anchored in smoother water about three miles from the beach, the Costa dell' Ambra. The sun had not risen very high when the whole fleet of ships, in ones, and pairs, and sections, was ordered in from the outer roads.

" To lie at ' short stay ' with engines ready sounds like a leisured proceeding, but it was anything but that aboard the ships. I am sure no express stevedoring ever began as quickly or was continued at such a pace. With us, disembarking our people was no great task as our men had stout legs and their gear and equipment were light and handy, but the big carriers of the fleet had a vastly more difficult job. . . . One large transport (we had noticed her making very heavy weather of it on the day before—her ' jumbo ' derricks being aloft and ready in conditions that would normally have called for deck stowage

and maybe an extra lashing or two) was anchored near us, and I would say that her cable was hardly wetted before she was listed a few degrees under the outboard weight of a sizable tank. I felt rather proud of the Red Ensign when I saw that tank dangling overside for a few minutes before a large tank-carrying craft got alongside to take delivery."

About this time two or three violent underwater explosions rocked the ship—sappers were blowing up a ridge in the beach which obstructed the landing craft. The disembarkation went safely on, the infantry-carrying craft letting go a stern anchor while some moderate distance from the land and then steaming slowly on. Often the current swung them a trifle sideways, but whatever happened it was in no time that the soldiers were

running over the ramp and up the beach and disappearing beyond a walled and cultivated patch. Tanks and mobile artillery went ashore next, often lurching and keeling at the water's edge. But these, too, got safely off and purred away into the country beyond. Doing so they demolished the stone wall, the stones of which were then built into a pier for small boats. During the afternoon Captain Bone's ship left for Malta.

The merchantmen which came from the Middle East were loaded with trucks, guns, bulldozers, ambulances, etc. A Master who saw merchantmen anchored off Alexandria and was stirred by the sight, speaks of his surprise that no bombing occurred after an enemy reconnaissance aircraft had flown over. Nor did any air attack occur during the five days' voyage to Tripoli. In an encounter with a submarine, however, a vessel was lost.

The total number of ships and craft of all kinds used in the landings was 2,700, most of them self-propelled landing craft. It was the greatest armada the world had known. One ship's Master said that, in a sense, it reminded him of Henley Regatta and added that, despite the numbers, he had experienced more trouble in Birkenhead Dock.

No bombing occurred during the first day, but thereafter air raids at night were frequent. Some vessels were lost from this cause and near misses were numerous, but the total shipping casualties were an infinitely small percentage. Not a single troopship was lost or damaged. Unloading the first convoy took three days— a docks group of specially trained soldiers sailed in each ship—and it was to the speed and excellence of this work that a part of the immunity to loss and damage was due.

Fourteen British hospital ships and five hospital carriers were used. From the beginning they were on the spot, taking casualties from the landing beaches. The carriers were fitted with craft which could take on wounded at the water's edge and, on reaching the carrier, be hoisted on the davits. One hospital ship was sunk by enemy bombs. Merchantmen also took men away from the island—prisoners of war.

But the Sicily landings were not the end, but only the beginning of the Mediterranean victory. Salerno and Anzio came after and the campaign which led to the liberation of Rome ; and the work needed in taking troops and equipment to the newly occupied islands of Sardinia and Corsica. To Italy have gone hundreds of thousands of troops and vast quantities of equipment, mainly in British and American ships, but also in ships flying the flags of most of the United Nations. The crews of many of these ships have been in the Mediterranean for months on end, and, so far as some of the coasting ships go, even for years. Much of the work has been unspectacular but none the less vital.

18. The Return to France

On June 6th, 1944, hundreds of ships of the Merchant Navy stood off the coast of Normandy bringing, along with ships of the Royal Navy and Allied merchantmen, the British and American armies to liberate France. A number of small vessels flying the Red Ensign in these French waters had been among the ships which brought our soldiers out of Dunkirk. For them it was a glorious return. For the Merchant Navy as a whole it was a culmination of its work. Already it had taken part in several great amphibious operations—North Africa, Sicily, Salerno. This was the greatest of them all. And as it was the greatest, so it was in some ways the most triumphant. The expedition was more hazardous than its predecessors, for the enemy's resistance was known to be thoroughly prepared and deemed strong. Moreover, weather was uncertain, and had led to a postponement for 24 hours. Yet, in the result, our losses in ships were fewer than in North Africa, Sicily or Salerno ; over the first fortnight they amounted to less than one per cent. of the total tonnage employed.

In all more than two-thirds of the merchant tonnage, flying many flags, was under British control. This mighty host of ships crossed the English Channel almost with immunity, safe under the guard of aircraft and warships, and placed the armies ashore at the appointed time. Coasters of all sizes actually beached themselves on French sand, coming off again on the chosen tide. And from D-Day onwards a shuttle service of ships to and fro across the Channel proceeded with great

THIS IS THE DAY. The shadow at the top right is the coast of France. The endless pattern on the sea is the Merchant Navy. Landing-craft shuttle back and forth between the beach and the supply ships anchored in the distance ; others weave among those unloading under the balloons in the foreground. The Allied armies are ashore and advancing. This is their reservoir of power.

COVERED BY THE NAVY and the Allied Air Forces the closely ranked merchantmen unload their stores in waters unruffled by enemy bombs. Losses from enemy air attack were negligible.

regularity. In a war that has held many surprises, this success at such small cost is one of the greatest. It was due first to perfection in organisation and planning; second, to skill and resolution on the day; and third, to the enemy's faulty perception and growing weakness both on the sea and in the air. Our command of the sea round Europe, which had been steadily growing for a year, was shown to be approaching the absolute.

Preparations for this invasion began in 1942, when, appropriately enough, some of the very cross-Channel ships that sailed to France during peace, and others which used the Irish Sea, were fitted as infantry assault ships. Coasters, which have played such a valiant part, began to have their masts strengthened and heavier derricks fitted. In that year also, the United States chartered

to us some small passenger ships for use in this operation; these were sailed by British crews over the Atlantic, although not without loss from enemy or storms.

During 1943, plans were pushed ahead. Thirteen fine cargo ships building in America were changed over for use as assault ships carrying infantry, and transferred to the British flag. Ports were surveyed in detail, and at many of them oil tanks and pipe-lines were laid down. Later, stocks of bunker coal were quietly installed ready for the day when they would be used for the ships in the operation. Over a thousand coasters were examined for speed, range, and ballast needs, and finally hundreds were taken in hand for special preparations. New coastal tankers were built for bulk or cased petrol, and enormous amounts of gear were ordered—

nets and slings for lifting vehicles, equipment to fight fires.

Thus were ports, ships and material planned. What of the seamen? They were now to embark on an operation where peril would be as commonplace as before, but in which normal time and overtime would be indivisible, and leave perhaps impossible. A " V " scheme which made these facts clear and gave some compensation for them was worked out, and officers and men were asked to volunteer. The response was fine. Many thousands were employed in the operation —about 25 per cent. of those who volunteered —while a further percentage were held in reserve to replace casualties or men being rested. Happily, casualties were lighter than had been feared, totalling rather less than a hundred in the first month.

Coasters which had never carried anything more exciting than coal or potatoes between Liverpool and Ireland, found themselves working under that hall-mark of adventure, Combined Operations, carrying out beaching exercises and learning to beach without broaching-to. As D-Day grew nearer— though still several months off—7,000-ton infantry assault ships rehearsed taking aboard and landing the selfsame troops they would transport to France. As one sea captain said : " We grew so schedule-minded that, if we were five minutes out, we thought the war was lost ". Throughout this period, of course, American armies and material in mass were being brought across the Atlantic by British, American and Allied merchantmen, and our coaster fleet was, in addition, still stocking the south of England with coal and commodities, turning it into a sort of granary against the time when normal transport would be severely curtailed.

This invasion differed from former landings in that, although the Merchant Navy was worthily represented, the spearhead was formed, in the main, by White Ensign landing craft. The short sea voyage allowed these little ships to carry men and tanks in great convoys and strings across the Channel, so

OVER THE SIDE goes the white-starred army, down on to the rain wet decks of the landing-craft rocking alongside in the choppy sea.

THE MERCHANTMEN LIE CLOSE IN TO THE SHORES OF FRANCE. BEHIND THEM ARE FIVE \

that a merchant captain of a 7,000-tonner carrying infantry described himself as sailing past ten miles of them, milling round and bawling their heads off. It was as if, he said, he were going down a waterways Strand. In previous operations, the big cargo ships had borne a variety of material, but now, in the early stages of the build-up, they took M.T. (mechanical transport) and nothing else so that they could load in a day and discharge in a day. (Yet to say " nothing else " is misleading for they often took 500 troops, stowed away in odd corners with an ingenuity only seamen and soldiers can contrive. In

similar fashion, coasters took other vital units.)

The stores, including ammunition, were borne in coasters, four-fifths of which had normally carried coal. Many now carried something even more combustible—petrol. Independence of mind and character is a trait of the Merchant Navy and the small coaster above all has her own way of doing things ; yet they now sailed with the precision of men-of-war, and it was only abounding honesty which led a blunt skipper to say, when asked how he was getting along after making four voyages with petrol, that he " wouldn't be sorry to get back to coal ".

OF WAR AT SEA. THE BEACH BEFORE THEM IS WHERE THE ROAD TO THE LAST FRONT BEGINS

Their work was invaluable for, taking ton for deadweight ton, the small ships can put on the beaches almost twice as much material as the big ships. Thus, in many ways, it was a small craft job, as Dunkirk had been.

Merchantmen in the forefront on D-Day and immediately afterwards were as varied as the work they did. The full story of the coasters and of the part they played will be told elsewhere. Of the deep-sea vessels taking part, the experience of a personnel ship is typical.

The *Empire Rapier* (Captain Walter R. Edmonds) sailed at 6 o'clock on the evening before D-Day carrying some 1,500 British troops and came to anchor at 5.10 a.m. next day, some miles off the coast of France. Her master had attended conferences which continued for two days or more and in which every arm took part—Navy, Army, Air Force, and War Transport. " The right stuff in the right place at the right time " was the keynote. Moreover, on this ship Montgomery's axiom at El Alamein was followed —-to everybody down to ships' boys the plan was explained. They were told also that this was the first invasion of its kind for 900 years and, although this might have savoured of a romantic attitude to facts, they were left in no doubt that they were making history.

During the voyage the wind had been westerly and fresh, the sea moderate for big ships, but rough for small. The moon was at the full and at times bright, but some cloud was in the sky.

Tension was naturally high as the ship sailed her slow course to France and, for a part of the voyage, down a mineswept channel no more than 400 ft. wide across which a 3-knot current was flowing. The route was as firmly charted as a main highway and, indeed, contained two points which seamen were soon calling Piccadilly Circus and the Hub of the Universe. During the voyage the ship had overtaken large numbers of L.C.T.s bearing tanks, but the time came when they passed her in turn.

As the voyage reached its close, ships for the American beaches and the other British beaches became visible, advancing inexorably and serene and turning from dim ghosts to a clearly limned armada as night broadened to day. The ship's company had heard during their voyage a roaring in the heavens as our aircraft had swept to France, and about an hour before anchoring had seen a glow in the sky from the air bombardment. To this was now added the nearer concussion of salvos from the battleships and the sharper reports from destroyers, so that one or two small coasters felt they were lifted clean out of the water.

As they drew close, all was in readiness. The troops, all true shipmates by reason of many rehearsals, had breakfasted at 3.30 a.m. —the men on this ship had dry hash and grilled bacon and a ship's tot of rum. The ships had learnt to come to an anchor and lower boats within ten minutes. The sea swell was troublesome, and a 6 or 7-foot rise and fall is difficult to strike with a flat-bottomed L.C.A. lowered from the davits. One or two sister ships had a worse time, and did not get all their landing craft away without some small damage to themselves, but the troops, some of whom had been sitting in landing craft for an hour or two before they set their feet on dry land, were got safely away. In launching the heavier L.C.M.s (landing craft mechanical) stewards often lent a ready hand, afterwards turning up to serve the ship's lunch in white jackets as if nothing unusual had occurred.

As the *Empire Rapier* lay at anchor two 6-inch shells flew in her direction, but neither came within dangerous reach. While the ship was still off Normandy, the Yorkshire troops she had brought had already penetrated two or three miles inland. The Brigadier in charge of them wrote to pay tribute both to Royal Navy and Merchant Navy, generously saying that the fact that his objectives were so well reached was due almost entirely to the splendid send-off the ships gave his men, adding " our casualties during the landing stage were remarkably small ". The *Empire Rapier* has made further voyages to France without mishap, but that does not mean that her Master and crew undergo no strain. For one thing sleep can be short. In those first days Captain Edmonds had little or no sleep for 56 hours, and on a quiet journey commonly goes sleepless for 23 or 24 hours.

No justice can be done to the individual adventures of the host of merchantmen engaged ; some caught glimpses of tank battles and air bombings ashore ; a few struck mines ; many came under shellfire from shore batteries ; most of them underwent bombing at night. In their later visits to the beaches they saw ships as closely assembled there as at Cowes Regatta ; and ashore they saw repair shops, and airfields at work.

Forty-two Red Ensign tugs have worked off the French coast, and a large number of others, flying the White Ensign, or Dutch and American. They have done a score of jobs—towed over ammunition barges and rescued L.C.T.s.

One tug, the *Empire Folk* (Captain Arthur Hall), found herself taking part in the invasion almost by accident. She did not know what was afoot, and on picking up a disabled L.C.T. and asking a destroyer where to take this landing craft was surprised by the laconic answer : " To France ". Captain Hall makes no reference to astonishment in his report but he notes that he " passed several floating mines ".

It was on June 20th that tugs went post-haste to France to deal with ships driving ashore in a nor'easterly wind that grew to a full gale and lasted, with little respite, for six days. The weather throughout had not been kind, but this storm was a grave interference. Its likelihood, judged by weather records taken over 70 years, could have been put at no more than a third of one per cent.; but here it was, and nothing but heroic efforts in unloading when the wind and water abated —efforts in which ships' crews took a full share—kept supplies going.

But even before that, the crews' work in discharging ships had led a chief officer to say " We are seamen and soldiers and dockers, too ". They had done all they could ; that fact stamped the whole endeavour. Off the French coast, for instance, Sea Transport Officers added to more normal duties by assisting in beaching craft and piloting others to anchorages ; in British ports one or two similar officers worked a week on as little as 15 hours' sleep and others tramped stone quays till, when they sat down, they could hardly rise again.

It was this sort of devotion which enabled the ships to achieve their quick turn-round—cargo ships filled with M.T. were sometimes discharged on beaches in ten hours—and which kept the shuttle service going with its convoys, its swept route controlled like a lane of traffic, and its reserve of ships. As the invasion became more firmly established and armies and supplies increased, so did the number of ships grow. And this is the true measure of the problem—that the task does not diminish after D-Day. A stiff task grows stiffer.

EPILOGUE

Once, in a life, when unprepared,
Death fronted us with talons bared,
And dared you venture . . . and you dared.

Twice, in a life, your hearts and hands
Have kept us among living lands
When other props collapsed as sands.

By your endurances, our race
Stands steady in the slippery place
Where glory tramples on disgrace.

JOHN MASEFIELD.

Printed in the United States
69358LVS00004B/35